FAITH, FACT AND FANTASY

C. F. D. Moule is Lady Margaret's Professor of Divinity at Cambridge University; P. R. Baelz is Dean of Jesus College, Cambridge; John Wren-Lewis is a mathematical physicist in the Research and Development Department of Imperial Chemical Industries Ltd.; D. A. Pond, M.D., F.R.C.P., D.P.M. is a consultant psychiatrist at University College Hospital and the Maudsley Hospital, London.

Faith, Fact and Fantasy

C. F. D. MOULE
J. WREN-LEWIS
P. R. BAELZ
D. A. POND

Collins

FONTANA BOOKS

First issued in Fontana Books, 1964

*Printed in Great Britain by
Cox & Wyman Ltd., London, Fakenham and Reading*

PREFACE

The 'Open Lectures' of the Cambridge Divinity Faculty have recently taken on a 'new look'. Instead of a weekly lecture by a single lecturer throughout a term – a plan which seemed to justify itself for many years – the new pattern has come to be a much shorter course of three or four lectures, each delivered by a different lecturer. The series in Lent 1963 on *Objections to Christian Belief* drew unprecedented crowds, partly, no doubt, because of the personality of the speakers, but partly also because of the theme and the treatment. In an atmosphere of free inquiry, only shortly before the impact of the Bishop of Woolwich's *Honest to God*, there were many who might have shown extreme impatience with any statement by Christians that even hinted at complacency or self-defence, but who were struck by the sight and sound of Christians engaging in the frankest self-criticism. The lectures, when published, were paid the compliment of a parallel volume of self-criticism from the non-Christian side – *Objections to Humanism*.[1]

The present series, delivered in Lent 1964 and maintaining the attitude of free inquiry, attempted to face certain basic questions. Does science destroy belief? Is God real? Has psychiatry replaced religion? Is Christ unique? Two of the four lecturers were deliberately chosen as professionals in fields other than theology. John Wren-Lewis, a research scientist in Imperial Chemical Industries, was

[1] Both sets were published by Constable in 1963.

already well known to many for his published lectures and articles and for the considerable part that he plays in *Honest to God*. About Dr. Desmond Pond, a consultant psychiatrist at University College Hospital, it is pleasant to recall that, over twenty years before, as an undergraduate of Clare College and President of the Student Christian Movement, he triggered off the whole series of 'Open Lectures' when he approached Dr. J. S. Whale, then President of Cheshunt College, to ask whether he would be willing to give the first.

The 1964 lectures, for the most part just as they were delivered, are now offered to a wider public.

C. F. D. Moule

CONTENTS

ACKNOWLEDGEMENTS

The authors and publishers wish to thank the
following for permission to use quotations:
Faber & Faber for lines from T. S. Eliot's
The Confidential Clerk and *The Family
Reunion*; and S.C.M. Press for Paul van
Buren's *The Secular Meaning of the Gospel*.

DOES SCIENCE DESTROY BELIEF?

by

John Wren-Lewis

Why do people go on thinking that science has in some way undermined religion? The persistence of this idea is profoundly irritating to theologians and other apologists for religion, for there are dozens of books about, many of them by scientists, which prove conclusively that no scientific discovery or theory about the way things work can possibly contradict the religious interpretation of the meaning of life as a whole. The conflicts of the past three hundred years, say the theologians, were misunderstandings, brought about by the arrogance of some scientists who thought they had the answers to all life's problems, and the narrow-mindedness of some religious authorities who insisted on tying their faith to out-of-date scientific ideas. But the very frequency with which books appear (to say nothing of articles and sermons) putting this point of view forward bears eloquent witness to the fact that the general public remains unconvinced; indeed, the idea that science has rendered religion out of date is probably stronger and more widespread than it has ever been, in spite of the fact that few ecclesiastics now identify themselves with out-of-date science, and few people today expect science to solve all human problems.

This would be an intriguing social phenomenon even apart from any direct interest in religion, and in fact an understanding of it takes us to the heart of some of the most fundamental problems confronting our whole society.

Irritated theologians sometimes say that the whole notion of science rendering religion out of date is merely a rationalization of people's desire to avoid the responsibilities of religion, but that is altogether too superficial a view of the matter. Even if there were any truth in the charge, it would still beg the enormous question of why people did not make use of this rationalization until about four centuries ago. Prior to that, although there was no dearth of systematic and sophisticated study of nature, it was almost universally taken for granted that such study led on naturally and inevitably to the religious interpretation of the meaning of things – that

> In contemplation of created things
> By steps we may ascend to God

as Milton's Adam put it in *Paradise Lost*. There were violent differences between different religious interpretations, but no sense amongst the general run of scholars of a possible conflict between religion and 'natural philosophy'.

This arose only when the study of nature began to be permeated by an entirely new outlook from about the sixteenth century onwards, and the truth is that this outlook has changed the whole character of human life. In science itself it brought about the revolution which has been described by an eminent Christian historian, Professor Butterfield, in his book *The Origins of Modern Science*, as a major mutation in human affairs compared with which the other revolutions of the history text-books are beginning to look like mere minor displacements. Science started to shoot forward in a quite unprecedented way, in spite of the fact that the people engaged in the study of nature were no cleverer, no more mathematically-minded and no more capable of acute observation than those who had practised

12

'natural philosophy' before them; this amazing advance, Professor Butterfield argues, came about because, and only because, people developed 'a new feeling for matter'. But this new outlook had other effects too, throughout society, and in some ways the sense of conflict between science and religion is symptomatic of them all.[1] I believe this is what Sir Charles Snow was getting at when he described British society since the scientific revolution as the scene of a clash between two quite different cultures, two 'ways of responding to life' – but the dichotomy goes far wider and deeper than the failure of communication between science and humanities faculties in British universities, with which he was mainly concerned. It affects people throughout the world, educated and uneducated alike – indeed to some extent we are all split personalities because of it – and it involves people's deepest feelings, not just their intellectual habits and convictions.

To understand this conflict it is necessary to go beyond any of the attempts that have yet been made to characterize it. It is the literary historians who have given most attention to this question and most of them have tended to use words like 'disinherited' or 'rootless' to describe the new outlook

---

[1] Sir Isaac Newton, one of the great pioneers of the scientific revolution, was himself still able to take the traditional view. 'The business of Natural Philosophy is to argue from phenomena,' he wrote, 'and to deduce causes from effects, until we come to the very first Cause, which certainly is not mechanical.' But already by this time the change had begun to set in: in fact, there is a decidedly polemical note in this statement ('. . . which *certainly* is not mechanical') that would have been quite unnecessary in earlier ages – and of course the world had already seen Galileo's clash with the Inquisition, and heard Erasmus warn the Church that it was identifying the new learning with heresy in such a way as to make orthodoxy synonymous with ignorance.

13

associated with science and technology. Mr. T. S. Eliot has spoken of its emergence in the seventeenth century as a 'dissociation of sensibility'; Miss Kathleen Raine speaks of a loss of the perennial human tradition of supernatural symbolism; and other critics talk of people severing their contact with mankind's psychological roots in nature.[1] Snow approaches the question in quite a different way, with a strong bias in favour of the new outlook, and he makes the important contribution of seeing the experimental method of modern science as a crucial factor. In order to see the connection between these two approaches, however, and to see their full significance, it is necessary to appreciate more about the nature of the experimental method than most people (even most scientists) do.

It does *not* mean 'proving your theories by experimental test'. It is a commonplace in philosophy that nothing can ever be proved by experimental test, because an infinite number of tests would be required. What you *can* do is to *disprove* theories, and the essential feature of the experimental method is that it sets up artificial situations especially designed to disprove the chosen theory if possible. This, and this alone, makes radically new departures and developments in theory possible, but it carries an implication – namely, *that experience is itself reliable knowledge in a sense that none of our ideas can ever be*. Now this is just what is alien from mankind's traditional outlook on life. Most people in most ages and most civilizations have assumed, not as a result of argument, nor even really as a result of inherited tradition, but almost by immediate feeling, that the world known in experience is only a veil for

[1] I have attempted a detailed survey of this subject of the changed situation of the arts in an article in *The Critical Quarterly* for May, 1960, entitled 'The Decline of Magic in Art and Politics'.

deeper realities 'beyond' or 'behind' it, and that the object
of all human efforts, whether scientific, artistic or religious,
must be to penetrate beyond the veil as far as possible.
Modern technology itself provides an excellent analogy in
the picture on the television screen, which is perfectly con-
sistent in itself yet still only an appearance, a realm of
'phenomena', being continually produced by some quite
different power behind the scenes, which might well stop
producing it at any moment. Bishop Berkeley would surely
have made great use of this analogy, and indeed his latter-
day disciple, Professor D. M. Mackay, has done so to great
effect in his own efforts to present a modern apology for the
religious position. Mr. T. S. Eliot has done the same thing
by employing the cunning of poetry to recapture the feeling
of the traditional outlook: in his play *The Confidential
Clerk* he makes a character say:

> I want a world where the form is the reality
> Of which the substance is only a shadow –

and in an earlier play, *The Family Reunion*, he has a
chorus which expresses the traditional human feeling about
the world of ordinary experience as vividly as I have ever
seen it expressed:

> We do not like to look out of the same window, and see
> quite a different landscape.
> We do not like to climb a stair, and find that it takes us
> down.
> We do not like to walk out of a door, and find ourselves
> back in the same room.
> We do not like the maze in the garden, because it too
> closely resembles the maze in the brain.
> We do not like what happens when we are awake, because

it too closely resembles what happens when we are
asleep.
We understand the ordinary business of living,
We know how to work the machine,
We can usually avoid accidents,
We are insured against fire,
Against larceny and illness,
Against defective plumbing,
But not against the act of God.
We know various spells and enchantments,
And minor forms of sorcery,
Divination and chiromancy,
Specifics against insomnia,
Lumbago, and the loss of money.
But the circle of our understanding
Is a very restricted area.
Except for a limited number
Of strictly practical purposes
We do not know what we are doing;
And even, when you think of it,
We do not know much about thinking.
What is happening outside of the circle?
And what is the meaning of happening?
What ambush lies beyond the heather
And behind the Standing Stones?
Beyond the Heaviside Layer
And behind the smiling moon?
And what is being done to us?
And what are we, and what are we doing?
To each and all of these questions
There is no conceivable answer.
We have suffered far more than a personal loss –
We have lost our way in the dark.

Does Science Destroy Belief?

Mr. Owen Barfield makes the same point by reference to a different kind of art when he throws out the suggestion, in his book *Saving the Appearances*, that the coming of a new outlook on the world at the time of the scientific revolution was shown up in the new use made of perspective drawing at the same historical turning-point. The common assumption that earlier artists were simply not clever enough to draw in perspective will not, he argues, stand up to examination. Careful study of the detail of Egyptian or Greek or Byzantine or medieval art will show that the technique was certainly there, but it was never developed – and Mr. Barfield suggests that this was because people just did not *feel* that the world was a realm of individual objects 'in the round', since they saw everything as a symbol or 'appearance' of deeper realities beyond.

Such an outlook on life can have no place for the experimental method, for it will seem impious or dangerous or both to try to alter the general pattern of 'natural' experience, and it will seem silly to allow experience, which may well be unreliable, to override any really authoritative interpretation of the hidden causes of things.[1] Books on the

[1] It is sometimes suggested by classical scholars that only the Platonic tradition in European thought was really incompatible with experiment: Plato's view that our world of experience is no more than a shadow on the cave-wall is often contrasted with Aristotle's requirement that theories should 'save the phenomena'. But 'saving the phenomena' is worlds away from the experimental method: history should have taught us by now that the ingenuity of the speculative intellect is such that almost any theory can be made to save the phenomena with a little trouble – witness Ronald Knox's famous 'proof', with the aid of anagrams, etc., that Queen Victoria was the true author of *In Memoriam*. Even Occam's Razor (the rule of not multiplying explanatory 'entities' beyond necessity) is only a very partial safeguard against this sort of thing, *unless* it is

history of science are apt to tell the story of how Galileo's detractors refused to look down his telescope at Jupiter's moons, as if it were a simple case of Galileo's unbiased desire for truth confronting a wicked obscurantism, but the fact is that the detractors were completely justified by their own lights, and by the tradition of the whole human race up till then. If experience is a mere veil, it is absurd to the point of impudence to suggest that the sight of a few specks of light through a piece of glass could possibly call in question an interpretation of the hidden forces underlying planetary motion, on which the best minds of the human race had worked for centuries. Galileo was proposing something more revolutionary than an alternative theory of planetary motion: he was proposing a new view of knowledge and of life, and this was the real reason why the Papal authorities saw him as a threat. They could have found an accommodation, in due course, with the Copernican theory of planetary motion – indeed the Pope had already authorized its use for calculating calendar revisions – but the *attitude* which Galileo advocated was one which threatened the very *raison d'être* of religion as revealer of hidden reality.

It also implied a revolution in social life, as Bertold Brecht was at pains to make clear in his play about the life of Galileo. The traditional outlook may be described as a

---

applied with the aid of rigorous, systematic experiment designed to render explanatory 'entities' redundant wherever possible – and this will simply not happen if the 'entities' are regarded as 'things in themselves', more real than the phenomena they are introduced to 'explain'. In relation to science as we know it today, therefore, the common allegiance of Plato and Aristotle to the notion of meta-physical realities 'beyond the physical' is more significant than the differences between them.

ritual outlook, not only in the context of specifically religious ritual but in relation to life as a whole, in that both work and social relationships are seen as part of a great ritual drama whereby people adjust themselves to the pattern of the hidden realities 'behind the scenes'. Perhaps the classic statement of this view of life is the well-known speech which Shakespeare put into the mouth of Ulysses in *Troilus and Cressida*: the 'degrees' of society are presented as part of the same pattern that runs throughout nature, since the human, animal and vegetable kingdoms all reflect the same hidden order of reality as the stars and planets:

> The heavens themselves, the planets, and this centre,
> Observe degree, priority, and place,
> Insisture, course, proportion, season, form,
> Office, and custom, in all line of order.
> And therefore is the glorious planet Sol
> In noble eminence enthroned and sphered
> Amidst the other; whose med'cinable eye
> Corrects the ill aspects of planets evil,
> And posts like the commandment of a king,
> Sans check, to good and bad.

With the decline of feeling that experience needs to be given meaning by reference to hidden realities beyond, the sense of ritual and the sense of 'degree' automatically began to decline as well, and this led both to the attack on specifically religious ritual in the Reformation and also to entirely new attitudes to the whole business of labour and social authority. Instead of seeing their work as a ritual cultivation of nature within the universal divinely-ordained pattern, people began to see it as a transformation of nature for the enrichment of human experience. The industrial revolution was not just a consequence of the scientific revolution, it was an integral part of it: modern defenders of the traditional outlook who are anxious not to cut themselves off from science sometimes speak of the technological application of science as a sordid exploitation of pure scientific truth for commercial ends, but in fact the *motif* of application is integral to the purest of pure science once this is based on the experimental method, since this involves treating theories as *formulae for communicating possible innovations* rather than as intuitions of deeper truth.[1] And along with the new attitude to work went a new attitude to social hierarchy and authority generally; Professor Stuart Hampshire expressed this extremely succinctly some years ago in an almost throw-away remark in a book review in a Sunday newspaper:

> . . . industrial progress depends on an ever-increasing diffusion of a scientific attitude and training, and this unavoidably spreads habits of irreverence, scepticism and unrestricted questioning to all levels of society. It is then too late to restore that inarticulate respect for customary authority that was indeed natural in a pre-industrial state.

So there may have been highly practical considerations,

[1] This view of the nature of modern scientific theory has become best known through the work of philosophers of science like P. W. Bridgeman who are more concerned with abstruse problems in the theory of modern physics than with technology, but the connection has been clearly seen by that *doyen* of philosophers of science, Professor K. R. Popper, in his paper, 'Three Views Concerning Human Knowledge', now reprinted in the volume *Conjectures and Refutations*. I am taking up an entirely different evaluation of the matter from Professor Popper's, however, as will become clear later in this lecture.

as well as purely religious concern, behind the Inquisition's desire to resist Galileo's ideas. Brecht puts a scene into his play in which a young disciple of Galileo agrees with the Inquisition's condemnation, in spite of believing Galileo's theories to be correct, because he feels that the loss of the idea of the world as the expression of a great invisible drama will make people unwilling to accept authority and unwilling to toil their lives away to maintain the pattern – and if this seems like dramatist's hindsight, it is worth remembering that Shakespeare, an even greater dramatist, expressed concern about exactly the same possibility, right at the beginning of the period when the new outlook was first making itself felt in the world. He wrestles with the theme again and again in his plays, and in the speech already quoted Ulysses is made to go on to argue quite explicitly that the loss of the sense of 'degree' will mean disaster:

O when degree is shaked,
Which is the ladder to all high designs,
The enterprise is sick. How could communities,
Degrees in schools, and brotherhoods in cities,
Peaceful commerce from dividable shores,
The primogenity and due of birth,
Prerogative of age, crowns, sceptres, laurels,
But by degree stand in authentic place?
Take but degree away, untune that string,
And hark what discord follows. Each thing meets
In mere oppugnancy. The bounded waters
Should lift their bosoms higher than the shores,
And make a sop of all this solid globe,
Strength should be lord of imbecility,
And the rude son should strike his father dead,

21

Force should be right, or rather right and wrong,
Between whose endless jar justice resides,
Should lose their names, and so should justice too.
Then every thing includes itself in power,
Power into will, will into appetite,
And appetite, an universal wolf,
So doubly seconded with will and power,
Must make perforce an universal prey,
And last eat up himself.

Today it seems to many people that this prophecy has been altogether too grimly fulfilled. Have we not great numbers of broken homes to witness to the fact that people no longer have any belief in a mystical sacramental bond in marriage 'behind' the personal relationship and the legal contract? Has not the loss of a sense of authority in parenthood, somehow rooted in the nature of things, brought about a spread of juvenile delinquency, sometimes perhaps to the point where the rude son strikes his father dead? Has not the disappearance of 'instinctive respect for customary authority' brought near-chaos to economic and political life, to the point where the only way to avoid all parties meeting in mere oppugnancy is for totalitarian governments and private enterprise advertising men to work on the principle that strength shall be lord of imbecility? Does not the decline of the religious sense of dedication to 'king and country' mean that states have to misuse words like 'justice', 'right' and 'wrong' to gain people's allegiance? Has not modern technology, with its loss of reverence for the natural order, brought us almost to the point where a war, or even an accident, could make a sop of all this solid globe? Even if we avoid nuclear destruction, does not the new order threaten to make life intolerable by despoiling the countryside, filling the air with clamour and finally choking the world with 'plurisy of people'?

A great many people who have no specifically religious axe to grind are led by considerations like these to join with apologists for religion in calling for a revival of traditional ideas of supernatural reality and cosmic order, and they are joined by still others who feel that the arts must inevitably be deprived of all depth and meaning if cut off from the ancient traditions of supernatural and cosmic symbolism. But this call is futile unless experimental science is to be completely given up, and few people would be prepared to ask for that today. In the centuries that have elapsed since Galileo's encounter with the Inquisition the essential rightness of the experimental method has been vindicated beyond question, not least in those very discoveries which make the modern world such a dangerous place. Those who ask for a recovery of the traditional outlook, whether explicitly, as in the case of the literary figures I mentioned earlier, or merely implicitly in the various books that seek to 'reconcile' the current scientific world-picture with the ideas of supernatural reality and cosmic order, are able to do so only because the gulf of incomprehension between the two cultures allows them to be ignorant of what their proposed world really means. This applies even to some scientists, for science itself is still taught largely in the classical idiom, at any rate in this country: it is taught, that is to say, as a system of ideas about the world, with relatively less emphasis on the methods by which these ideas have been arrived at and might at any time be changed. It is precisely because science teaching *is* still dominated by the classical outlook in this way that we suffer as much as we do from overcrowding of syllabuses and the consequent evil of ever-increasing specialization, for the 'systematic' approach to learning is inherently unsuited to subject-matter which is continually expanding – but that is another story. The point I want to make here is simply that the classical approach to the teaching of science allows even some scientists – and at least one distinguished philosopher of science, Professor K. R. Popper – to go on thinking of scientific theories as 'explanations of phenomena', in which the gods and spiritual forces of occult tradition are simply replaced by quanta, force-fields and the like, whereas a proper emphasis on *method* would make it clear that the modern theories are never more than models to suggest new lines of practical action, and therefore capable of being discarded at any time in favour of radically new models in a way which would be impossible if they were attempts to express the hidden truth behind phenomena. Experimental science succeeds by finding truth in experience, in action,[1] and this is utterly incompatible with the traditional outlook on the world, both logically and psychologically. It is

[1] Professor Popper argues very heatedly against the 'operationalist' view of the status of scientific theory, in his essay on knowledge to which I referred in the footnote on p. 20, precisely on the ground that it does have the effect of equating science with technology and hence of lowering scientific investigation from a proper cultural activity to a sophisticated kind of plumbing. This seems to me to miss the very thing about modern post-Galilean science which is distinctive, namely that it succeeds because it raises 'plumbing' to the level of a genuine cultural activity, instead of regarding all practical action as an inherently inferior, rather dirty business, to be kept as closely in check as possible by ritual discipline. Professor Popper's own great insight into the nature of experiment, namely that it is a method of disproof rather than of proof, seems to me to point in precisely the opposite direction from that which he himself has decided to take in this particular essay.

in this sense, rather than because of any specific discoveries or theories, that science has completely undermined what is ordinarily thought of as 'belief', and all the attitudes to life that go with it.

It does not in the least follow, however, that the people who are perturbed by the decline of 'belief' are worrying about nothing. On the contrary, precisely because applied science has so vastly increased mankind's powers of manipulating the world, we need a compelling vision of the good of human life more urgently than it was ever needed before – and at the same time science itself, precisely insofar as it does concentrate more and more consciously on the provision of 'know-how', is of its very nature incapable of providing any such vision. There is a real dilemma here – but just as soon as it is squarely faced *as* a dilemma, the way between the horns becomes clear. So long as the issue is posed as a conflict between science and the new culture on the one hand, set over against the traditional outlook and art, morality and religion on the other, there is no way out, for compromise is impossible, and neither 'side' can be merely abandoned. When the dilemma is squarely faced, however, it becomes immediately clear that it is based on the unquestioned premise that because all our traditions of great art, morality and religion are rooted in the old outlook, they are necessarily dependent on it for their continued vitality: and once this premise *is* questioned, one fact stands out which makes it appear very questionable indeed, namely, that science too used to be rooted in the traditional outlook, prior to the scientific revolution, but the decline of that outlook certainly did not destroy science – it fulfilled it. Is there any reason at all why the same thing should not happen in relation to the other aspects of human life? Is it in any way logically necessary that a compelling vision of human good, capable of giving depth to art and a basis for human relationships, should be dependent on belief in occult reality or cosmic order? This is the nettle which the Bishop of Woolwich attempted to grasp in *Honest to God*, and that was why he found the book selling in hundreds of thousands instead of the hundreds which he originally expected.

I think the book has been widely misunderstood by the professional critics, even by some who approve of it, and one reason for this is that Dr. Robinson did not himself formulate the matter particularly clearly: he is not personally at all at home in the scientific world, as he remarks at one point in the text, and although he has had the wit and sympathy to see how the vast majority of people in modern society feel, I do not think he wholly feels with them himself. Thus he coins a most vivid phrase to express the kind of religious vision which our modern culture finds impossible – 'God out there' – but he weakens the force of his analysis by speaking of this as an 'image' of God, and suggesting that the modern world-view renders this 'image' out of date. He thereby lays himself open to the bland, totally uncomprehending criticism of the Archbishop of Canterbury's *Image Old and New*, that of course all images of God are inadequate, but it is better not to try to be too fashionable, since in the end of the day any natural image is better than a more sophisticated one. This misses the point completely, for in truth there is something much more profound involved than the fashionability or otherwise of an image. The point is that the new culture can see no meaning in using *any* image for realities 'out there', *because it has no sense of an 'out there'*: discussion about whether this or that image is a proper representation of the ultimate reality behind the scenes of experience seems utterly futile to most people today, *because they do not regard the world of experience as a scene.* Failure to formulate this issue clearly leaves the Archbishop and other traditionalist critics of the Bishop of Woolwich free to rest in the comfortable belief that the task of evangelism is to convert the modern scientific world back to a belief in 'God out there', and I am not sure whether even Dr. Robinson himself is completely clear about the utter impossibility of doing this. The fact remains, however, that where his traditionalist critics line up with his atheist critics in accepting the fact that the modern world-view with its emphasis on experience and action must necessarily be deprived of any vision of ultimate good worthy of the adjective 'divine', Dr. Robinson has staked a claim for the notion that this need not be so – that we can find all the important values associated with the idea of God, 'down here', in the world of experience itself. This was the one interesting thing that could be said in the present situation, and the sales of *Honest to God* show that it met with no small response, in spite of the fact that the book, intended primarily for scholars, is couched in theological jargon which can hardly make it easy reading for the general public, even the educated public.

Possibly the most important insight we can get into the way between the horns of the 'two cultures' dilemma – and one to which Dr. Robinson makes no reference, except insofar as he quotes from my own writings – comes from science itself, now that this has advanced into the psychological field and begun to throw light on the way human attitudes originate. I am referring to the insight which led Freud to diagnose religion as 'the universal neurosis of humanity'. Here again, religious apologists often try to dismiss this, but they are able to do so only because they

have not understood what is involved. When Freud called
religion a life of illusion he was not claiming to be able to
disprove any theological argument, or anything of that sort.
He was referring to the practical discovery, verified again
and again in actual psychological analysis, that when people
try to order their lives by constant reference to hidden
realities beyond experience, or by fitting into some supposed general pattern of things, they are always in fact
trying to escape from the full impact of experience itself,
and from the responsibility of taking a definite creative
stand of their own. The technical psychological term for
such a way of living is 'paranoid fantasy-obsession'; the
term 'paranoia' is commonly used in a more restricted
sense, to describe a state in which a man feels himself
persecuted by occult powers, but in fact there is no final
distinction between one sort of belief in occult forces and
another, for belief in occult powers which are benevolent or
neutral can easily pass over into belief in persecuting occult
powers with a slight change in the person's circumstances.
Freud's genius lay in perceiving that a paranoid attitude is
just as much a matter of escape when shared by a whole
society, on the basis of a highly articulated system of
mythology or theological doctrine, as it is when a lonely
individual becomes obsessed with persecution mania. An
individual who sees others primarily in terms of their
'degrees', their role in society's ritual drama, is just as cut
off from vital human relationship as is the 'social isolate'
who avoids contact with others on the ground that they are
engaged in a giant conspiracy against him. A culture which
restricts human creativity to the cultivation of the natural
world within the limits of a set pattern, on the ground that
this pattern reflects the will of higher powers beyond, is
just as much motivated by the desire to avoid responsibility

for the state of the world as is the frightened neurotic who lives by compulsive private rituals. In fact, the moral stability of societies governed by 'belief' (in the ordinary sense of that term) is not a safeguard of man's humanity, as modern defenders of the traditional human outlook usually claim; it is a stability *purchased at the price of inhibiting the expression of man's humanity.*[1] Science failed to develop prior to the scientific revolution (in spite of the fact that people just as able as any modern scientists were devoting themselves to the study of nature's work-ings) because this sort of activity was *inhibited by the traditional outlook, as part of a general inhibition of human creativity.*

This insight certainly does suggest that *any* activity which has anything in it of genuine human creativeness will be fulfilled rather than destroyed by the decline of the traditional outlook – and it is no mere coincidence, in my judgement, that the scientific revolution in Europe did in fact coincide with a great flowering of artistic creativity in the Renaissance. When artists in subsequent centuries felt themselves to be deprived of a significant role in society, in danger of being reduced to mere decorators trailing on the coat-tails of utility, it was not because they had been cut off from the traditional outlook, as critics like those I quoted

---

[1] The point is well made in that same scene of Brecht's play on Galileo to which I have already referred, when Galileo is made to exclaim with some impatience to his worried disciple that he does not *want* people to go on toiling their lives away in the vineyards in the belief that it is all part of the divine plan. They should irrigate the vineyards, and introduce machinery to make the work easier, Galileo exclaims – and the social order should be changed so that they and not only the few at the head of society can enjoy leisure and the fruits of the earth. 'But they are tired, Mr. Galileo,' replies the little monk.

earlier are wont to maintain, but rather because society had not pressed the revolution against that outlook right through to its logical conclusion in the realm of artistic activity as it had in the scientific and technical realm. It was still assumed by society generally that the work of the artist must necessarily be in some sense representational, which meant that if he was deprived of his traditional task of bodying forth symbolic representations of occult realities, the only role left would be that of copying the external *status quo* of the natural world. Wherever the revolution against the traditional outlook has been pushed right through, however, and the artist has consciously accepted the task of being genuinely creative in the sense of using symbols to express *entirely new possibilities of experience which man may use his scientific know-how to realize* (sensuous experience, emotional experience and social experience, in different proportions according to the kind of art) it seems to me that the creative energy of the Renaissance has been maintained, and with it the promise that the artist will find in the present century that the new outlook gives him, as it has already given the scientist, a role in life which is far more significant than his traditional one, rather than less significant. And this is true not only of the artist as a special kind of man, but of every man in so far as he is a special kind of artist.

What then does this insight mean for the question of moral vision, the vision of the good by which human creativity can be directed? One thing is certain – a non-paranoid outlook is by definition humanist, in the sense that it does not try to hold up any larger pattern beyond human life as a norm by which human action is judged. The trouble is that humanism up to now has been largely negative. It has undoubtedly provided a certain amount of creative moral inspiration, from Renaissance times onwards, which upholders of the traditional outlook are apt to ignore, but this has been almost entirely because it served to canalize the moral energies of a relatively small group of social reformers to work for the removal of positive inhumanities that had flourished under cover of organized religion and the appeal to 'degree' – inhumanities of which, incidentally, Shakespeare himself was fully aware, in spite of the speech he attributed to Ulysses: it is by no means without significance that he put this speech into the mouth of a man of ancient Greece – he himself had a much more equivocal attitude to the traditional outlook, as his other plays make clear.[1] But humanism needs to be something more than a mere assertion of the value of personal life and creativity, if it is to provide guidance for creativity and moral inspiration for enabling personal life to transcend the conflict of competing egoisms, and historic humanism has been notably unsuccessful in providing any such positive vision of human good capable of wide appeal to the general run of human beings. This is not, emphatically not, any reason for abandoning humanism and trying to recapture the traditional outlook in any form: to try to do this because of the dangers of modern civilization would be akin to the neurotic's wish to cling to his neurosis from fear of the dangers of full life. The truth is rather that, in this field as in the realm of artistic activity, the Renaissance failed precisely in so far as society failed to push the revolt against the traditional outlook right through, and here too it seems to me that we are today witnessing the gradual emergence

---

[1] This is very well brought out in Professor Danby's book, *Shakespeare's Doctrine of Nature*, and the point comes over the more forcibly in the light of the author's evident initial sympathy with the traditional view.

of a new vision which fulfils the Renaissance promise because it *does* complete the revolution.

We are witnessing, that is to say, the emergence of a deeper humanism based on a positive vision of human good in concrete experience, and it springs from the same discipline of psychological analysis that has exposed the neurotic character of mankind's traditional moral and social orientations. The ultimate fear underlying these orientations was that unless people conformed to a universal pattern, life would disintegrate because individuals would meet each other in 'mere oppugnancy'. When modern analytical psychology is applied to the practice of psychotherapy, however, the effect is precisely to induce people to face up to the possibility of oppugnancy, of conflict, in their personal lives, and to show them that they can find, on the other side of it, as it were, an experience of vital personal love which proves, as a matter of sheer fact, to be the goal towards which all our manipulations of matter and all our social organizations are directed, whether we are aware of it or not.

Now in this experience of love as a concrete ultimate good it seems to me that we have in fact *an experimental counterpart of religious belief*, on the basis of which religion can be fulfilled just as science has been fulfilled. Freud used the term 'religion' as a simple synonym for preoccupation with occult powers and the wish to live by fitting into a universal hidden pattern, and this was understandable enough, since the vast majority of religious apologists do so too, but in fact many things point towards the possibility that religious ideas and images may, like those of science and art, find a valid and far more significant use in referring to experience and potentialities for creative action. This is the proposal which the Bishop of Woolwich has put forward in general terms, but because his terms *were* so general his argument at this point has failed to carry conviction with a lot of people: both atheists and traditional ecclesiastics have joined in objecting that his use of the word 'God' to indicate simply that the most real things in life are personal is redundant, since it adds nothing to the position of the atheist humanist. Freud's own analysis, however, points towards a more compelling possibility: he was so impressed with the central creative role of love in human life that in spite of his avowed atheism he used a religious term to describe love in his book *Civilization and its Discontents* – he referred to 'eternal eros'. No doubt he meant this as a figure of speech and no more, but I believe this sort of figure of speech tells us more about the experience of love than more prosaic figures which refer to love as a feeling, an urge or even a relationship. It points towards the same characteristics of the experience of love that makes romantics employ expressions like 'falling *in* love' or say that 'this thing is bigger than both of us'. To take these expressions seriously as the basis for a way of living may be folly, but for that very reason they are certainly not redundant. Moreover such a way of life would be religious, in the sense of involving faithfulness to a vision of ultimate good as concrete, personal being, yet it would not be paranoid, since it would be rooted in experience and continually subjected to verification in action, with the consequent possibility of falsification.

I believe such a way of life would be the fulfilment of religion in the sense that the great doctrines of one religious tradition at least – the Jewish/Christian tradition – were *originally formulated for this sort of purpose, rather than for the neurotic purposes to which they have subsequently been put*. It is a well-known fact that many of the great prophetic figures of the Bible and early Church spent more energy on attacking religion than on defending it, and their attacks were by no means directed only at obvious corruptions and abuses, or rival brands of religion: they often attacked their fellow-Jews or fellow-Christians, on the ground that the original faith was being totally distorted. Moreover their descriptions of the process of distortion often anticipate Freud's analysis of the paranoid outlook quite directly: it was not mere nostalgia that made Freud feel a strong sense of kinship with the Jewish prophets. The whole Biblical prophetic tradition was based on the commandment forbidding 'graven images' of God, and Jewish commentaries make it clear that this was not concerned just with crude idols of wood and stone: it was held to forbid mental images as well – yet there was certainly no intention to restrict true religion to intellectuals capable of high abstract thought, and indeed the very people who most insisted on the commandment were quite uninhibited in their actual use of expressions like 'King', 'Judge' or 'Father'. This makes sense only if the purpose of the commandment was *to prevent the idea of God, and any descriptive images associated with it, from being referred to hypothetical occult realities*. An idol is an image or an idea to which people are compulsively attached, and such compulsion comes about as soon as the image or the idea is regarded as the only way we have of knowing a supreme reality beyond experience. The prophets could use their anthropomorphic images freely without any such danger of taking them too seriously because, and only because, they used them in the same kind of way as the modern scientist uses his models, namely to refer to reality that is directly accessible in common experience for the images to be checked against. And the Biblical writers in fact leave us in little doubt on this score, if we once examine their statements without reading back our preconceived ideas into them. Although they insist that God cannot be seen, they use language which clearly indicates experience rather than what we have come to think of as 'belief'. 'Taste and see that the Lord is good', is a typical statement, and Jesus of Nazareth spoke of having recovered the true Hebrew faith in God from the distortions imposed on it by the Jewish religious authorities of his day, by saying of himself and his disciples, 'We speak that we do *know*, and testify what we have *seen*.' There is also ample evidence, if we once let the Biblical writings speak for themselves, that statements like these were not meant to refer to special 'mystical' experiences, but rather to the common experience of love. St. John is particularly emphatic on this point. 'If a man says, I love God, and hateth his brother, he is a liar' – but '*Everyone* that loves is born of God and knows God' – for 'God *is* love'. But in this St. John is doing no more than echo the central tradition of prophetic Hebrew religion, which was expressed by one Rabbinic commentator in the expression 'God dwells in our togetherness', and by another in the statement that the *shekinah*, the glorious presence of God, is found between husband and wife in marriage.

Undoubtedly there are plenty of places where the Biblical writers seem themselves to be employing the idiom of the paranoid outlook, but it is important to remember that *in those days there was no other idiom for them to use*, even for the purpose of telling people to break free of that outlook and live by their experience. Many ideas and activities which suggest paranoid attitudes to us would have an entirely different connotation in cultures already ruled by the paranoid outlook. Puritanism and asceticism, for example, which in our culture almost certainly denote a wish to escape from spontaneous personal relationships, could in traditional cultures have sprung from the precisely opposite desire to break sufficiently free from the compulsive ties of 'degree' and 'natural community' to be able to enter spontaneous personal relationships.[1] Jesus' words about the need for a man to hate his family in order to follow him seem to us like a harsh demand for total dedication to 'religion' in the Freudian sense, but in societies where people thought of themselves as cells in the social body rather than as individuals, the pursuit of vital personal love might on occasions seem to involve just this kind of ruthless break with family ties. Indeed, the experience of finding vital personal relationship with another individual would seem, in such societies, to make a man or woman stand out above nature, and might well seem to demand description in terms of 'super-natural divine power', whereas we automatically take such terms to refer to occult reality, because we see the whole world of experience as perfectly 'natural'. Perhaps the most crucial example of this general point is to be found in the declaration of the early Christian Church that the Absolute Reality had come into this world from the world beyond in order to destroy the veil between this world and the world beyond; this is probably the only kind of statement that could be made, in a world wholly governed by the paranoid outlook, to convey the need to abandon that outlook in favour of taking experience absolutely seriously.

In fact, I believe we may say that the decline of the paranoid outlook which has been taking place in our

---

[1] I have attempted a detailed analysis of puritanism in this light in an article entitled 'The Passing of Puritanism' in *The Critical Quarterly* for January 1964.

civilization over the past three hundred years represents *in itself* a fulfilment of one of the most important objectives which the prophetic figures of the Bible – including Jesus himself – were trying to achieve. Freud's notion of mankind suffering from a universal inhibition of its humanity, a universal bondage to the illusion of fantasy-life, is after all itself a very Biblical idea, the idea which later theology named 'original sin', and it would have seemed no strange suggestion to the Biblical writers that the general run of religion is bound up with this disease ('conformed to this world', as St. Paul put it). They did not, in other words, condemn the paranoid outlook *only* because it distorted religious ideas: they condemned it as an integral part of their positive religious endeavour, which was to liberate people from the illusions of 'this age', from 'bondage to sin', so that they *could* find the Supreme Good in experience. Consequently I do not think it can be mere coincidence that the first large-scale decline in the paranoid outlook has taken place in Christendom, in the wake of the one prophet in all history who ever claimed that he had won an absolutely decisive victory over the power of this world. He did not himself suggest that the general liberation of mankind from superstitious bondage should follow immediately; he expected his revolution to be suppressed by people who used his own words and expressions for the purpose; but he claimed to have planted a mustard-seed of liberation which would grow secretly, influencing men's minds in all sorts of subtle unsuspected ways, until it flowered in places where it was least expected. This seems to me to point directly forward to the modern world, and it is interesting to note that Jesus' famous denunciation of the distortion of religion in his own day, 'The Sabbath was made for man and not man for the Sabbath', implies just the same sort of revolution against the traditional outlook on life as does the modern world's practice of basing science on the principle that theory is made for experiment, not experiment for theory.

Up to a point, therefore, I am happy to agree with the atheist humanists who say that Christianity is now out of date, although I would hold this view for a very different reason. I would say that the 'good news' of liberation which the first Christians proclaimed is out of date because the liberation is to a considerable extent an achieved fact, so that it is no longer news. (Some humanists, notably those who have been influenced by the psychological ideas of Dr. C. G. Jung, would actually come very close to this way of looking at the matter, in that they would describe Christianity as an important factor in the past psychological growth of the human race.) Where I differ totally from the atheist humanist is in believing that there are other elements in Christianity (and in other major world religions too, I am inclined to believe, although I am not sufficiently knowledgeable about other religious traditions to be definite about it) which can still be of the highest possible importance in providing an empirically-based faith for living in the new world which lies before us. This is what the much-discussed task of 'de-mythologizing' the Bible and other religious writings really amounts to – discovering the empirical truths underlying the mythological statements which were originally made to convey these truths to people living under bondage to the paranoid outlook. For example, interpreted in this way, the notorious Christian description of God as trinity-in-unity, which causes puzzlement or ridicule when applied to the ordinary idea of God as a great Master Mind behind the scenes, may be seen as a very penetrating formula for distinguishing between the genuine experience of creative love and various sub-personal relationships which can easily masquerade as love, although there is no life in them. The traditional formulations are couched in the language of more patriarchal societies than ours, but the meaning is not hard to express in terms which are completely intelligible today. They tell us that love, when we really know it, is such that the images of Fatherhood, Sonship and Spiritual Procession can all be simultaneously applied to it: in other words, unless a relationship is a threefold unity in which every person involved performs equally the roles of initiation, acceptance or suffering, and overflowing interpretation, that relationship is something less than a genuine experience of the creative reality of love.[1]

I must add at this point that although I think this sort of exercise in re-interpretation can be of great importance, I am dubious about how far it is desirable to press the attempt to 'save' traditional formulations. For example, the traditional statement of the Christian doctrine of the Incarnation which I quoted a moment ago (summarized in the credal assertion 'He came down from heaven') should probably now be discarded, since it preserves the idiom of the paranoid outlook from which I believe it was meant to rescue people, and unless one kicks away the ladder one has climbed up there is a permanent temptation to slide down it again. But one traditional religious doctrine which undoubtedly does still have something of immense importance to say in the modern world is the doctrine of God as creator of the world *ex nihilo*, and it is with this that I shall conclude.

[1] For a more detailed analysis on these lines, see my article entitled 'The Doctrine of the Trinity' in *The Listener* for 11th May, 1961.

The first thing to be said about this doctrine is that it is in no sense, as is almost universally assumed today, the starting-point of Christian belief. The common habit, in Sunday-school books and academic treatises alike, is to define the foundation of Judaism and Christianity as the revelation that the hidden reality behind experience is a single Creative Mind, upon which subsequent revelations have erected a picture of the character of that Mind; but this story simply does not square with the historical facts, even apart from any of the considerations I have been putting forward. One of the major features of the history of Judaism and Christianity alike was the struggle against various sects and movements which held that the natural world was too impure and evil to be God's creation – a view which simply could not have arisen if the word 'God' were *defined* in terms of creation of the natural world. If, on the other hand, the idea of God originated from the experience of creative love in personal life (a conclusion much more in line with the findings of modern anthropology) then Tennyson's question 'Are God and nature then at strife?' arises at once, for the system of nature as we ordinarily experience it has no place for such personal values as love, beauty or justice. Against this background, the assertion that nothing exists apart from God's creative action becomes *a supreme declaration of faith in man's ability to change the world if he acts upon it in the power of love*: there is no *thing*, no systematic order, apart from personal action – only potentiality.

In the Book of Genesis this faith is expressed in the statement that the world is the sort of place over which man can and should exercise dominion. This is as far as can possibly be imagined from the conventional religious view of the world as a great divinely-ordained system into which man should fit himself, but it is very much the faith implied in the modern technological outlook. Few scientists or technologists would think of describing their work in these terms today, so debased a coinage has religious language become: but our modern feeling that physical life need not be futile, that diseases can be cured and so on, is irrational to the point of absurdity if we merely weigh man's power against the odds that face him on a naturalistic basis. Whether we acknowledge it or not, our technological confidence is rooted in a *real* sense of the 'super-natural': the proponents of the traditional outlook are actually using a completely misleading term when they talk about 'recovering the sense of the supernatural', for if 'supernatural' is identified with 'occult', then by definition people cannot ordinarily have any *sense* of it. Modern man, on the other hand, would probably want to avoid using the term 'super-natural', because he takes all experience, including his own experience of creative action, as perfectly 'natural', but if the term 'sense of the supernatural' has any meaning at all it is surely applicable to the ability which we assume in practising science and technology, to stand *above* the ordinary course of nature and thereby change it. And in the early days of the scientific revolution some of the pioneers did in fact see their work in these terms: for example, Francis Bacon made deliberate use of the mythology of the Book of Genesis to describe applied science in the *Novum Organon:* 'For man by the Fall fell at the same time from his state of innocency and from his dominion over nature. Both of these losses, however, can even in his life be in some part repaired; the former by religion and faith, the latter by the arts and sciences.'

Since that time, it seems to me that the Genesis-faith in man's ability to exercise dominion over nature has been vindicated, both by the undoubted success which technology has achieved and by the discoveries of pure science, which has more and more revealed the ultimate structure of the natural world to be a matter of probabilistic rather than systematic order – 'no-thing' in itself but an infinite potentiality for making 'things'. Our great need today, I believe, is to recover that faith as the conscious basis for our continuing scientific and technological endeavour, for without it I think humanism will inevitably collapse in despair sooner or later. With it, on the other hand, we can go forward in the hope that personal life, lived on the Ground of Love, is indeed more real than anything else.

This was the hope which the Jewish faith originally expressed in terms of the myth of *general resurrection*, and which the first Christians believed had been vindicated by the resurrection of Jesus. I believe that as we come to understand more of the emergence of our new culture we shall find that this myth played an extremely important part in giving mankind its new-found confidence in the possibility of creative change in the physical world, and this would be true even if it were only a myth and no more. I do not myself believe there is anything that forces us to the conclusion that it was only a myth, however. On the contrary, it seems to me that when scientifically-minded people today dismiss the idea of resurrection as impossible in any literal sense, they are allowing themselves to be guided more by the sort of reverence for the inevitability of the *status quo* which characterized traditional culture than by the spirit of science itself. Paradoxically, the materialist scientist here aligns himself with conventional religion which has also tended to treat the idea of resurrection as a myth describing the survival of some occult part of the personality called the 'soul' in some other world behind the scenes called 'heaven'. It seems to me, however, that the general line of the actual findings of modern science make it quite reasonable to take the New Testament idea of *physical* resurrection quite seriously, if we look at them in the *spirit* of modern science (i.e. the spirit which recognizes that 'inert' gases can be made to form compounds, and bear seeds to grow in atmospheres which are supposed to be incapable of supporting life).

In the first place we now have definite evidence from physiology that the body's mechanisms for preserving its vitality and integrity are much stronger than we ordinarily realize, so there is no difficulty in imagining that they might be made to prevent ageing and to resist even major acts of violence (like crucifixion). Moreover if this were to happen, the result would not merely be *everlasting* life: people's whole experience of time would change, since we now know that the sense of time comes from measuring our cyclical processes against the base-line of our general non-reversible growth.[1] There is also some evidence from psychoanalysis that we suffer boredom only because we unconsciously see passing time as bringing us ever closer to death. So everlasting life would be *eternal* life, a life in which time and space would seem like opportunities rather than as overwhelming realities before which people must bow – and, given such transcendence of space and time, it is possible to imagine man's dominion over nature extending even to the 'resurrection' of the past. There is a real possibility, in other words, that the idea of resurrection might well be an expression of the ultimate achievements of technology – yet at the same time there is evidence that

[1] See Professor K. G. Denbigh's article 'Thermodynamics and the Subjective Sense of Time', in the *British Journal for the Philosophy of Science* for November 1953 (vol. IV, no. 15).

such ultimate technological achievement is not just a matter of science alone, since the functioning of our bodily defence-mechanism is very much dependent upon our psychology. A longevity-pill alone could not give eternal life; that would come only in so far as people achieve fully human life at the personal level, by building a community wholly rooted and grounded in love. Hence it seems to me that the faith we need for the age that lies before us is indeed the original Christian faith – that God, whose name is love, has begun the work of freeing mankind from bondage so that the whole universe may be raised into the kingdom of love.

Just what practical religious expression can be given to this faith is something that still remains to be worked out. This is a question on which it is possible to venture only a very personal opinion, and in my experience the traditional forms of Christian worship, from the Quaker to the Catholic, are too loaded with the neurotic associations of the past to be of any use at all. Yet I feel very strongly that we need a Church, a practical religion: the task now is to find it.

IS GOD REAL?

by

P. R. Baelz

Is God real? Questions of belief and questions of truth are of fundamental importance to the Christian faith. At the centre is belief in God, and the only ultimately satisfactory ground for believing in God is the fact that God really is, and that the belief is true. Belief in God may console or comfort the individual in his loneliness or on his death-bed. It may cement the cracks of a competitive and class-conscious society. It may afford us an imaginative vision of certain features and possibilities in our world to which otherwise we should have been blind. All this may or may not be the case; or it may be the case for some and not for others; or it may be the case today and not tomorrow. Suppose, however, that there comes a time – it may already have come – when we no longer need or desire the comforts and consolations of faith, when we can live and die as men who, in Bonhoeffer's celebrated phrase, 'can get along very well without God'. Even then God may still be God; and if belief in him is well-grounded, it may still be our joy and duty to worship and obey him for his own sake. Beliefs stand or fall by their truth, not by their utility. Christian beliefs are no exception to the rule.

Is God real? This sounds a straightforward question demanding a straightforward answer. Surely we know how to distinguish between the real and the unreal, between Santa Claus and Harold Macmillan, between the Regius Professor of Astrology and the Regius Professor of Divinity. Of course we do. Anyone, however, who can lisp the grammar of theological utterance will answer immediately and correctly that God is not quite like Santa Claus or Harold Macmillan, and that he is even more real, in an odd sort of way, than the Regius Professor of Divinity. He is '*ens realissimum*', Being most real.

Already words are on the move, and to keep our balance we are compelled to ask questions of meaning before we tackle questions of truth. (We may note in passing that it does seem a little odd that, if God is in fact supremely real, there should be so much doubt about his reality. The 'hiddenness' of God is a problem of his being as well as of his providence.)

For many today, belief in God and the practice of the Christian religion have little or no meaning. This could conceivably be nothing more than a problem of communication. Expressions of belief and worship may have become antiquated, and may no longer be in 'a language understanded of the people'. Meanings and manners change, and Christian writers and preachers may have been sleeping for the last few centuries like Rip van Winkle. If this is the case, then what is required is only a work of translation. Such a work may be laborious and even difficult, but with patience and imagination and goodwill it should prove possible.

It is fairly obvious, however, that the malaise is more deep-seated, philosophical rather than psychological. There are many who would argue that Christian beliefs have no meaning because, as a matter of logic and epistemology, they *can* have no meaning. It is not the case that atheism is true and Christian theism is false, but that both are meaningless. 'Today, we cannot even understand the Nietzschian cry that "God is dead!" for if it were so, how could we know? No, the problem now is that the *word* "God" is dead.'[1] It is little consolation to the theist to be told that the atheist is his companion in the same sinking ship, and that the 'don't knows' top the poll because the question about God makes no sense.

Various moves are open to the Christian believer at this stage in the game. He may say that something has gone wrong with the traditional language, that the word 'God' has been keeping bad company, has become infected and must be placed in quarantine, and that another word or words must be found to refer to the same reality which used to be referred to by the word 'God'. The belief will then be the same, but the expression of that belief will be different. Or he may say that there is nothing wrong with the word 'God', it still has a useful period of life, but that really it refers to something rather different from what everybody had previously supposed. What we need is to retain the old expression, but alter the belief so expressed. Or again, with the suspicion that some of his colleagues may be indulging in a smart piece of theological 'lifemanship', he may feel himself morally obliged to drop both the belief and its traditional expression, and to join the company of reluctant but honest agnostics. I leave to the last the unexciting and prosaic suggestion that, with some careful thought and patient clarification, it may appear to him both possible and necessary to retain the traditional belief and something very like its traditional expression.

It is difficult to be sure which of these moves some of our contemporary theologians are making. Phrases like 'the dimension of depth', 'the God within', 'ultimate reality as personal', 'the ground of our being', are not transparently clear. What is clear, however, is that many of these stem

[1] Paul van Buren: *The Secular Meaning of the Gospel*, p. 103.

from the tradition which, in modern times, goes back to the Dane, Søren Kierkegaard, whose ridicule of the idea that Christian truth can be set forth in terms of a dispassionate metaphysic still echoes loud and clear, and whose *cri de cœur* that 'Truth is Subjectivity' sends shivers of delight down the existentialist's spine and strikes chords of dismay in the logician's heart. However, it is now generally admitted that there is a sense in which there can be no religious truth which does not engage the passionate concern and commitment of the believer. Religious truth is not true unless it is true for me; if the God in whom I believe makes no difference to me, I do not *really* believe in God.

This notion that commitment plays an essential part in religious faith is one of the factors which have greatly influenced contemporary theology. Another is the growing realization and acceptance of the fact that God is not objective in the sense in which the natural sciences understand objects and objectivity, that he is not a 'God of the gaps', and that his existence cannot be established in any of the ways in which we might establish the existence of a distant planet or a sub-atomic particle or a primordial cosmic explosion. The existence of God is not a scientific fact, nor even a scientific hypothesis. The scientist has 'no need of that hypothesis'. Yet another factor is the Biblical theologian's renewed insight into the distinction to be found in the Old Testament between 'God' and 'the gods'. When we read that 'The Lord, the Lord thy God, is one', we are not meant to understand that God is just one among many gods, or even the only actual god in the class of possible gods, as in an identity parade there might be one and only one criminal in the group of possible criminals. God is not *a* god at all. To speak of 'monotheism' and 'polytheism' in

the same breath, as if they were both species of a common
genus 'theism', is to invite the retort that, if that is how you
use the words, then the Biblical belief in God has nothing
to do with theism at all. Furthermore, if the advances in
scientific knowledge have made us thoroughly sceptical
about the existence of one or more gods or godlings in the
world, and *in this sense* atheistic, we can, if we so desire,
quite happily number ourselves among the 'atheists' and
still profess the Biblical belief in God. The Biblical belief
in God is not necessarily tied up with a belief in supernatural principalities and powers.

We must, however, at this point enter a strong caveat.
Words are slipping under our feet again. We are not sure
where or how we stand. To call Christians 'atheists' is to
speak paradoxically. The paradox points to one aspect of
the nature of their belief in God, and that an important
one. At the same time it may conceal or distort other aspects
which are equally important, and which give an intelligible
meaning to the expression 'Christian theism'.

The sense of the significance of personal commitment for
our understanding of religious belief, and the distrust of
categories of objectivity, both metaphysical and scientific,
have led many contemporary theologians to explore the
area of subjectivity. Perhaps we have been looking for God
in the wrong direction. If we wish to discover him, perhaps
we should look within. Now there is a long religious tradition, far older than Kierkegaard, which bids us look for
God within the still centre of the human heart. This
tradition is to be found inside and outside Christianity.
Within the Christian Church it is perhaps especially typical
of the Quakers with their distrust of dogma, their worship
in silence and their appeal to 'the inner light'; and it is
probably no accident that a number of Quakers have

welcomed this kind of theology as expressive of a way of thought along which they themselves had long been quietly travelling. It is incumbent, however, on those attracted by such an approach, that they should face fairly and squarely questions of belief and questions of truth. Is there not a risk of losing sight of truth altogether in the alluring vistas of subjectivity? Is not an appeal to subjectivity itself a denial of the claims of truth? The one question which I wish to raise as sharply as I can is the question, what happens to Christian *truth* when we present the Christian faith in terms of the subjective? What happens when we follow the advice to 'look within'? Do we discover God? Do we discover, as in a mirror, only ourselves and our own experience? In discovering ourselves do we also discover God? Do we discover God as substantive or only as adjectival to ourselves? Is each one of us his own god? Are there as many gods as there are men?

In order to put these questions in their proper context I wish to sketch in outline two types of contemporary Christian theology which are both subjectivist but which differ from each other in one very important aspect. The first I shall call 'Radical Subjectivism'; and although I have in mind a type of theology rather than the work of any particular theologian, I offer as a striking example the recent book by Paul van Buren, entitled *The Secular Meaning of the Gospel*. The second I shall call 'Qualified Subjectivism', and I offer as an example of this the theology of Bultmann, perhaps the simplest and most lucid expression of which is to be found in his small book, *Jesus Christ and Mythology*.

There are two fundamental points to be noted about the position adopted by the radical subjectivist.

First, he is a philosophical empiricist in the tradition of

David Hume. By that I mean that for him there can be no assertions of fact apart from assertions of straightforward empirical fact, ones which can in principle be tested by ordinary common-sense or scientific methods of observation. If these methods of testing are inapplicable – and what other methods have we? – if what appears to be a factual assertion makes or could make no difference to anyone's experience, if it is compatible with any and every state of affairs, then it cannot be saying anything and cannot be a factual assertion at all. What is, is definable in terms of what can in principle be observed. Now what appear to be assertions about the Transcendent, about Being itself, about God, are, it is held, compatible with any and every state of affairs. They cannot be verified or falsified. They are therefore factually empty. What cannot be false cannot be true either. There is a logical, and not merely a psychological, reason for the meaninglessness of assertions about God.

Second, he does not proceed to throw religious utterances out of the house lock, stock and barrel on the grounds that they are *altogether* meaningless and illegitimate. Instead he avails himself of the fruitful notion that the meanings of words and sentences are given by their uses – just as, for example, one might say that the 'meaning' of a 'pawn' is given by the uses to which this piece can be put in a game of chess. He then goes on to argue that religious utterances which *appear* to be assertions of fact, but which clearly are not assertions of empirical fact, *really* have a totally different use from that of making assertions and consequently a totally different meaning. They may express human feelings, or attitudes, or decisions. They may be stories or parables which are psychologically helpful or practically illuminating. They may be a mixture of all these, and it is the task of the philosopher of religion carefully to sort out the many different uses. Human beings do many different things with words; they are not always imparting information. In using religious language they are not imparting information at all – least of all information about another world – it is a *logical* fact that there can be no other world! – they are reacting to the only world that there is, the observable world, taking up an attitude to it themselves and recommending this attitude to others. Since our attitudes to the world in which we live are a serious matter, religion is a serious business and religious language a serious way of talking.

Before drawing out some of the implications of radical subjectivism we may notice that there is nothing in principle objectionable to the believer in the view that religious utterances may not really be what they appear to be, that they may be used differently in different contexts, and that one cannot tell from their grammatical dress alone what particular logical function they are attending. In fact we shall never acquire a proper understanding of religious language – and what goes for religious language goes for religion itself – until we are more alert to these different uses to which it is put.

Not only is it true that there is nothing objectionable in this principle; it is also true that believers make use of it themselves, more or less consciously, far more frequently than non-believers give them credit for. For example, I doubt whether the words 'heaven' and 'hell' have ever been construed by believers as geographical places, however they may have been imagined pictorially; and when the Psalmist wrote the words 'If I go down to hell, thou art there also' he was certainly not thinking in terms of public transport and underground sightseeing. Or, again, when the no doubt legendary nonconformist minister begins his prayer with the words, 'Thou knowest, O Lord, that thy people long for thy presence', he is not reminding the Lord of what the Lord had perhaps forgotten, he is actually giving expression to the longing of the people for the presence of God. Or, again, when in the service of Holy Communion Anglicans use the ancient words, 'Therefore with angels and archangels and with all the company of heaven we laud and magnify thy glorious name', many of them, if asked, would say that they were not thereby implying a belief in the existence of angels or archangels, but were using the image of a whole concourse of heavenly beings to express the depth and inclusiveness of their worship of God. Or, finally, take as an example of religious logic, though not perhaps of religious sanity, the recently resurrected practice of ritual cursing. Now it is perfectly true that the words to be found in the commination service in the Book of Common Prayer are in the indicative rather than the subjunctive – 'Cursed is he that removeth his neighbour's landmark' – but the uttering of these words is surely not intended to publish information about a matter of fact, but to be a solemn act of cursing. If this were not so, curses would not have to be lifted as well as pronounced.

Believers are accustomed to using language metaphorically, symbolically, poetically. Where they are frequently at a loss is to know just where these processes begin and where they end. Are *all* apparent assertions about God and the supernatural to be treated in this way, or only *some*? And if only *some*, then *which*?

The radical subjectivist holds that *all* apparent assertions about God are to be treated in this way. To put it bluntly, God is no more. The word has lost its meaning, and the

Reality has vanished. Van Buren, for example, sums up this side of his theology in the principle: 'Statements of faith are to be interpreted, by means of the modified verification principle, as statements which express, describe, or command a particular way of seeing the world, other men, and oneself, and the way of life appropriate to such a perspective.'[1] The world, other men, oneself – but no God. How then can he still claim, as he does, to be standing within the Christian tradition? His answer is in terms of his attitude to the man, Jesus of Nazareth. This is made clear by his second theological principle: 'The norm of the Christian perspective is the series of events to which the New Testament documents testify, centering in the life, death and resurrection of Jesus of Nazareth.'[2] Leaving aside for the moment the question of what he means by 'the resurrection' of Jesus, we may say that for him Christianity is basically the adoption of the historical perspective and the way of life of Jesus, adding the comment that theology has been completely taken over by ethics.

His treatment of God and of Jesus, and of the relation between the Father and the Son, comes out clearly in his exposition of one of the verses of the Fourth Gospel, in which Jesus says: 'He who has seen me has seen the Father; how can you say "Show us the Father"? Do you not believe that I am in the Father and the Father in me?' Van Buren comments: ' "Father" is the word which Jesus apparently used frequently in cases where his contemporaries might have used the word "God". It presents all the problems which arise when we try to analyse the word "God". The further explication of this word, however, is not the only, nor even the best, way to understand this passage, for the

[1] op. cit., p. 156.
[2] op. cit., p. 156.

56

passage itself suggests a *via negativa* of an odd sort. The author asks us to stop "looking for the 'Father'", for we shall not find him and the quest is beside the point in any case. Silence is the first and best answer to questions concerning the "Father". There are many "gods" and many "lords", but for those for whom the freedom of Jesus is contagious, who have been so touched and claimed by him that he has become the criterion of their understanding of themselves, other men, and the world, there is but one "Lord": Jesus of Nazareth. Since there is no "Father" to be found apart from him, and since his "Father" can only be found in him, the New Testament (and this passage especially) gives its answer to the question about "God" by pointing to the man Jesus. Whatever men were looking for in looking for "God" is to be found by finding Jesus of Nazareth.'[1] Forget the question of the correctness of his Biblical exegesis, concentrate on what van Buren is saying. For him Christian belief in God the Father not only involves commitment to the historical perspective of the man Jesus, it *is the same thing as* such a commitment. There is no movement through the Son to the Father, for there is no space, logical or theological, left in which to move.

It would take far too long to mount a full-scale critique of radical subjectivism. We must content ourselves with one comment and one question.

The comment is this. The radical subjectivist has to assert that the whole tradition, both Christian and non-Christian, of a 'communion with God' has been completely misconceived. If there is no God, there can be no communion with him. Something with the same outward form as that of practising the presence of God may continue, and may possibly have an important place in the radical

[1] op. cit., pp. 146–7.

subjectivist's life; but it will be little more than a man's quiet reflection with himself over the problems which confront him. To quote van Buren again: 'With his newspaper in one hand, to put it figuratively, and his Bible in the other, he tries to read the first in the light of the second, and perhaps he will also find the second opening his eyes to new aspects of the former.'[1] This is finely expressed, and such quiet reflection may indeed form a part of the traditional Christian's prayer. But if it is the whole truth, even about the puzzling practice of intercession, and if adoration is nothing but a cry of amazement, and thanksgiving a squeak of delight, then the experts in the art of prayer, saints ordinary and extraordinary, have been sadly at sea in understanding what they were about.

The question is this. Suppose that we ask the believer *why* he takes the perspective of Jesus as his norm and *why* he commends this norm to others. The answer, however fully developed, will be phrased ultimately in terms of its appeal, what van Buren calls its 'contagiousness'. Men will find the way of Jesus liberating, healing, enlivening, satisfying. Again, this is so obviously the sort of thing that believers do say when they commend to others the way of Jesus, that we may be tempted to accept it as a wholly adequate and satisfactory answer. But what is this contagion? Is it only psychological? Suppose that someone does not want to be liberated, healed and enlivened in this way; or does not find this liberation, healing and life in the way of Jesus. Suppose that the historical perspective of Jesus does not 'come home' to a man today in the same way as it 'came home' to the first disciples after Jesus' death. What are we to say then? Are we going to admit that there are other historical perspectives and other points of view, and

[1] op. cit., p. 189.

leave it at that, and *feel content to leave it at that*? Is the
unity of God to be broken up into a thousand, or even two,
different points of view? Van Buren admits that his own
exposition of the Christian faith is just such a point of
view, and reflects certain presuppositions which he himself
happens to have as a child of his age. He claims for it no
more. He would accept, I imagine, Santayana's dictum that
religions are not true or false, but better or worse. Are we
prepared, however, to give up claims to truth so easily?
When believers assert that Jesus is the *Way,* and couple
with this the assertion that he is also the *Truth,* are they
not saying that the perspective of Jesus is something more
than one possible way of seeing the world, one possible
way of responding to life; that it is in some sense *the* way
of seeing the world if the world is to be seen as it really is,
that it is in some sense *the* way of responding to life if the
response is to fit the realities of the situation? Again, are
they not saying that Jesus' way of life is somehow grounded
in his acknowledgement of the reality of God, and that his
freedom for others and for the world is one side of the coin
of which the other is obedience to his Father? It may not
be easy to understand quite what they are saying when they
talk like this. I suggest, however, that they are not merely
reiterating their own or Jesus' personal attitude to life in
other more impressive, more religious words, but affirming
that there is, as it were, ontological backing for such an
attitude. A claim to such ontological backing for the life
and person of Jesus seems to me to be an essential part,
not only of Christian belief which can properly be called
Christian, but also of the self-understanding of Jesus as it
is portrayed to us through the Gospels. When the radical
subjectivist claims to adopt as his norm the historical
perspective of Jesus, it is in fact a grossly distorted form of

this perspective which he has in mind. Jesus without Jesus' heavenly Father simply is not Jesus.

Radical subjectivism of this kind may be called a Christian humanism, but the accent will fall heavily on the humanism. To say that such a philosophy of life is not Christian in the full and traditional sense of that word is, I know, not to say that it is necessarily false, nor that it is not to be recommended, nor even that it is not the best 'religion' that we can have. However, before we dig deeper into the problems of Christian truth, I wish to take a look at what I have called 'Qualified Subjectivism'.

Qualified subjectivism shares many characteristics with radical subjectivism. It recognizes the world of objects as the province of the natural, historical and psychological sciences. It draws attention to the fact that man has to choose his attitude to the world, and that in this choice he expresses and experiences his freedom and responsibility. Man is not just an object for scientific observation and study, not just a thing to be pushed around. It can be truly said, in the language of Heidegger and Bultmann, that man has an 'existence' which, as it were, 'stands out' from the natural world, in which his freedom as a subject replaces his nature as an object. Now it is in this 'existential' realm that those religious utterances which are not straightforward assertions of empirical fact have their anchorage. Christian faith is a response of man to the world in which he lives, an 'existential' response in which he comes to a new understanding and a new realization of himself. So far the paths run parallel.

It is at this point that the important distinction between radical and qualified subjectivism occurs. The qualified subjectivist maintains that in this realm of existence, as contrasted with the realm of nature, man encounters God.

He cannot realize his own true self, he cannot become truly free, unless he recognizes the fact that his own true self is a gift to him from God and that his own true freedom is grounded in a response to the gracious act of God. Sometimes the same point is put in rather different language, namely, that to live freely is to live not in bondage to the fixed inheritance of the past, but to live confidently and courageously in openness to the future. To live from the past is to live as part of nature, to live from the future is to live from God.

Such language is admittedly metaphorical and analogical. Nevertheless it is used to describe a fact of experience which, it is claimed, can not be analysed away, the meeting or encounter or confrontation between man the subject and God the Subject. God reveals himself to man, and man knows God, at the point at which man acknowledges his destiny to live in freedom and love and discovers that he can live thus only if he receives this freedom and love from God. This belief in God involves two factors, the assertion that God really is, and self-commitment to him. The assertion that God really is is an assertion of a fact of experience, although not of what we have previously called a straightforward empirical fact. It is given its meaning and validity by reference to the area of human existence as known from within. In this area a man can *know* the reality of God. The existence of God is as objective, that is, as real as the existence of anything else which gets in our way. It is non-objective in that it does not belong to the world of objects known through sense-perception.

A corollary of the qualified subjectivist's location of the reality of God in the realm of human existence is his insistence that all assertions which appear to be about the relation of God to the world of objects must be interpreted as in fact about the relation of God to human subjects. What appear to be cosmological assertions must be interpreted existentially. For example, to say that God is the Creator of the world is not to say that God is responsible for the world, that it depends on him as on a First Cause. It is not to say anything directly about the world at all. It is to say that God does and will give to those who believe in him the courage to live out their lives as free men, which is the proper mode of human existence, *whatever the worldly circumstances or pressures may be.* Or again, to say that God raises men from the dead is not to say anything about the resurrection of human beings to some future life, but to say that God gives new hope and confidence in this life, *even when men are at the end of their tether.*

Qualified subjectivism is very attractive to the contemporary Christian. On the one hand it gives full scope to scientific procedure and knowledge, admitting the omnicompetence of the sciences in the field of all that there is to be known about the world. It rules out talk about the interruptions of the natural order by agents or forces from a supernatural order, and asserts that the use of this sort of language is the use of mythological, pre-scientific categories of thought. It accepts man's limitations as a part of nature, a creature of time with a life-span of threescore years and ten. On the other hand it maintains the real existence of God; it points to 'the God within' (yet not as a part of man, adjectival to human existence, but as a Subject to be encountered within human existence, and so to be addressed in personal modes and spoken of in personal categories); it joins in an unbreakable bond man's knowledge of God with his knowledge of himself; it grounds man's commitment to Jesus in a recognition of and commitment to Jesus' God, and it makes room for a good deal of Christian prayer and worship. We may well ask ourselves: have we not here sufficient of the traditional and sufficient of the modern to justify our calling it *the* contemporary expression of Christian belief?

Furthermore, do we not, by adopting a theological approach such as this, solve the problem of the nature of the relation of God to the world, and the still more difficult problem of the reconciliation of belief in the goodness of the Creator with the obvious pain and evil in the world, by ensuring that they simply do not arise? The sphere of nature and the sphere of human existence are quite separate. God does not operate in nature, but only in the sphere of human existence. Therefore he has no relation to the world, and is not responsible for its imperfections.

This sounds too good to be true. And so I believe it to be. The reason for my disquiet lies precisely in this absolute dichotomy between the areas of nature and of existence, and of the confinement of God to the latter. What is valuable as a distinction is unsatisfactory as a dichotomy. It is of vital importance to emphasize man's freedom and responsibility, to underline the fact that he is a subject, and not merely an object to be moved and manipulated as any other piece of the world's furniture. On the other hand, he is not pure spirit. He may 'stand out' from nature, but he is a child of nature. He may be free, but his freedom has been fashioned out of dust. His very freedom is intertwined with the forces of nature, so that a natural mischance can destroy his rationality and his responsibility. It is this fact of man's humble, natural origins which tempts some, mistakenly, I think, but quite understandably, to deny that man has *any* freedom or *any* responsibility and can be completely described in terms drawn from the natural sciences. A credible account of the origins and characteristics of man must, it seems to me, make room for elements both of continuity and of discontinuity in man's relation to nature. What God, or Evolution, has joined together, let no philosopher put asunder!

This disquiet is also concerned with the status of the God encountered in human existence. Is this God anything more than part of the natural order which is the basis of man's freedom and subjectivity? Is the phrase 'an encounter with God' merely a metaphorical way of talking of an uprush of the unconscious, or a release of psychological energy? Admittedly it would be a trifle odd to pray to the Unconscious, but is the practice of prayer and worship really compatible with this strangely restricted God? Furthermore, does this God provide solid grounds for human hope and courage? If 'nature' is in no way under his management, may not 'nature' in the end defeat him? To say the least, the hope that Love will ultimately triumph over nature is confronted with the fact of human death and the possibility of cosmic disaster, and although such hope is undoubtedly heroic and exemplary, it is open to the charge of unfounded optimism unless the God in whom it claims to trust is not a finite power, a part of the process of becoming, like the god of John Stuart Mill, or even, I suspect, the god of John Wren-Lewis, but a God who is, in the beginning as well as in the end, alpha as well as omega, ultimate and eternal.

My final comment on qualified subjectivism is that it is *prima facie* attractive, but basically unstable. It must either relapse into the humanism of the radical subjectivist, or press forward along the road which leads to a conscious metaphysic.

Before inviting you to follow me along this way, where shrieks of meaninglessness and groans of neurosis assail the pilgrim's ears, let us just check the equipment which we have already acquired. We acknowledge the appeal to experience and are wary of taking any step which seems to lead 'beyond' experience, for fear of entering an unknown world of make-believe in order to protect ourselves against the reality of the world we know only too well, a make-believe world in which anything can happen and anything can be true because we are its creators. We also agree that the question of God is inseparably bound up with the question of Man, that there can be no theology without a correlative anthropology. If Man is treated as merely one object among a number of objects, if his creativity, his sense of freedom and responsibility are denied, it makes no difference whether they are denied in the name of Nature or in the name of God. To reduce the stature of man until he is no more than part of the divine machinery is just as ill-conceived as to reduce him to nothing more than a part of natural machinery. The claim that theology is really anthropology in disguise, that there is no God, only Man, cannot be met by denying the humanity of man and calling him a worm. To vilify the creature is hardly the way to glorify the Creator.

So with fear and trembling, to metaphysics!

In actual fact, what I want to do is not to lay before you a complete guide to metaphysical theology, but to point to three areas in the discussion so far in which metaphysical questions have already raised their ugly heads, and to probe these questions a little more carefully. These are: first, the appeal to experience and the suggestion that there might be non-objective, transcendental facts of experience as in the qualified subjectivist's experience of God; second, the instinctive desire which we noticed for some ontological backing for our moral choices; and third, the strangely persistent practice of worship.

First, experience. We have accepted the appeal to experience, and so to experience we must go. But *whose* experience? Yours? Mine? Our experiences are not the same. Of course they are not; but is not the appeal to a *common* experience, to the same given ingredients out of which each of us makes his own private pudding? But *what* exactly is this common experience? I very much doubt whether there is any such thing as a *purely given* experience, such that it is not already distilled through human categories of interpretation. Experience does not expose itself in its nakedness, and facts are not simply offered to us on a plate. It is all 'a blooming, buzzing confusion' until we learn by attention, discrimination, trial and error to put some sort of order into it. Even the commonsense world of perception is an acquired habit, an interpreted world. If we go on to ask what the world is really like in itself, and not what it is like as we have ordered it, we may be tempted to describe it in the language of physics, believing that we have thereby discounted our apparatus of perception, and call the world of physics the 'real' world, and everything else make-believe. If this 'real' world of physics lacks many of the characteristics of colour, sound and smell, which in our ordinary moments we ascribe to tables, orchestras and mutton chops, perhaps we are compensated for our loss by tracking down reality to its lair. The theory of relativity, however, has brought back interfering man right into the heart of the world and language of physics. We simply cannot remove our interpretative categories in order to see what the world is really like apart from them, as we might remove a pair of dark spectacles in order to see what the world is like in ordinary light. Thus the question what is the world like in itself, or what is ultimate reality like, looks like a question which can never be answered. We can never know. And if we can never know, the sooner we leave off such vain questioning the better.

Perhaps from the observer's point of view alone we can never know. But is man only an observer?

Let us approach the same set of questions by another path. I wish to suggest that our active response to the reality which somehow is over against us is both psychologically and logically prior to our perception and understanding of the physical world. For example, the baby learns to see the physical world around him in process of trying to adjust himself to whatever reality there is. His seeing the world is part of his coping with it. If this is so, then the fundamental question to be asked about reality is this: what sort of response, or responses, does reality evoke from us, what sort of attitudes does it countenance and support? However much we may be responsible for the interpreted world as it appears to us, we cannot *do* just as we like. We are responding to something. Now no one in his senses wants to deny that the knowledge based on observation really does help us to respond to reality, but is the type of response on which this observational knowledge is based the only response appropriate to reality? Or does reality engage us in other ways which prompt us to speak of other sorts of facts than those which can be observed?

To come back to earth. Most of us for most of the time operate with two interpretative categories, 'things' and persons', each of which is linked with a different basic response. Are these enough? Or are they one too many? After all, there are some people whose world of experience seems to leave no room for persons – at least in the sense in which we ordinarily distinguish between persons and things, and think it appropriate to adopt different attitudes to either. We say that they treat persons as if they were things.

This brings me to the second point, what I called the instinctive desire for some ontological backing for moral decisions. Now the obvious thing about my making a moral decision is that it is a decision and not an inference, and that it has to be made and not deduced. Again, *my* decision is something that *I* have to make, and it cannot be made for me. Having happily admitted all this and summed it up in the tautology that my decision is free and mine, I want to go on to suggest that there is another side to the coin of free moral decision, namely that of obligation or duty. We do not simply *decide* our moral attitudes, as we might simply decide, after due consideration, which bottle of wine to drink with our chicken. We recognize a *claim* on us. The underprivileged and the outcast do not exercise a claim upon our compassion and help because we decide that this is to be so, but because we see that it is so. This insight is not a deduction from the observed facts, but it does rise out of the observed facts. It is potentially a decision to make a particular response to the observed facts, but this response is grounded in the recognition of a claim present in the observed facts. When people talk about Absolute Values in face of the clear evidence that different peoples and different ages have different values, when they write odes to Duty as well as compose hymns to Love, it is this element of unconditional claim which they have in mind. It is something which, they believe, confronts them in moments of making moral decisions. After psychologists and sociologists have done their best to explain our sense of duty in terms of natural and social pressures, this specific feature still eludes their grasp.

This element of unconditional claim is something that has to be taken into account in any attempt to understand reality. It is as real as the stone against which we stumble is real, and it can stop us in our tracks as effectively. It is in this sense a fact, based upon the analysis of our moral experience. It is possible that others may lack the experience which we analyse in this way. This does not prove that we are deluded or mistaken. Equally we cannot prove the others mistaken. They lack the evidence on which we ground our assertions. We can convince them of the truth of what we assert only if, by good fortune or by providence, they come to share our experience and see things in the way we see them. In all this there is implicit an appeal to experience – to one's own experience, tested and confirmed by the experience of others. As the methods of testing can never be impersonal, but necessarily involve a person's own response, there can be no universal proof. It is this fact which prompts people to talk of values as 'subjective', meaning by this that they are a matter of taste, and to refuse to speak of moral facts and moral truth. They are 'subjective' in the sense that they are discerned by methods which involve the whole person, but they are not matters of taste.

It might seem wise and circumspect to stop at this point with a dualism of what actually happens and what ought to happen, the world of observable fact and the equally real, although ontologically peculiar, world of value. I say 'ontologically peculiar' because this world of value, although in a sense an ideal world, is also real by virtue of the pressure which it exercises upon us in moral experience. I wish, however, to take another step, and to come to my third point, worship.

'Worship' is a vague word, and covers a multitude of different feelings, affirmations and practices. I am taking it to mean a man's total response to the reality which, he believes, he is 'up against'. The character which he ascribes to this reality will govern the nature of his worship. Christian worship, defined as well as offered through Jesus Christ, is a response which is not a manipulation of things, moving matter around in space, nor a recognition of a moral and impersonal claim, like the half-sensed presence of the forbidding arm of the law, but which, while making room for all this, is a response of love and joy and trust and gratitude based on the recognition of an ultimate reality which is itself loving, exuberant, trustworthy and gracious.

When we speak of worship we usually think of all the weird and wonderful antics which men have performed under the auspices of this word, the trappings of worship, and we are on our guard. The human mind has an infinite capacity for self-deceit. Candlelight and music and King's College choirboys may make us fancy that we have entered the presence of God and have heard his voice, when in fact we have only been bemused by the sight of the Dean and the sound of the organ. Because of this danger of deception, *all* worship has sometimes been dismissed as incantation, and it has been argued that we ought to settle the question of belief in God before we even begin to adore or to intercede. This sounds plausible, but is, I believe, fundamentally mistaken. In the first place, not all who worship, and believe that in their worship they are brought into communion with God, can be dismissed as idle dreamers. The cap simply will not fit. However, there is a second and more pressing consideration. If I am right in thinking that belief in God and a worshipful response to life, in the basic sense in which I described it earlier, are different sides of one and the same coin, then we cannot ultimately justify the belief without our being engaged in the worship. Worship is the seed-bed of theology – just as the making of moral decisions is the seed-bed of ethics. We must be as honest as we can in our worship as in our theology, and there will be a continuing interaction between them both. Moreover, theology is not restricted to the experiences of worship. Nevertheless, without experience theology remains speculation.

Christian worship, then, is a man's total response to the ultimate reality revealed to him through Jesus. It is not an alternative to the scientific or the moral response. It claims to unify and to fulfil these responses. Just as the truly worshipful response completes and integrates the scientific and the moral response, so in an attempt to express in language the ultimate reality in which our science, our morality and our worship are all grounded, we use the name of God. Observation and nature yes; moral decision and duty, yes; but inclusive and ultimate, in our response and in our language, worship and God. In God the ultimately real all penultimate realities cohere. What is and what ought to be are one.

Belief in God is inescapably metaphysical because it is belief about what is real in itself. The Bishop of Woolwich is himself a metaphysician when he writes with admirable lucidity: 'The question of God . . . is concerned with whether one can speak of *ultimate* reality at all and with what character this reality has.' He goes on to say that the true atheist, such as Marghanita Laski, would answer 'No', and agrees with her that this is 'the real dividing line between those who can speak of "God" and those who cannot'.[1] My own comment here would be that Marghanita Laski must be an atheist because she denies the possibility of metaphysics, but there are also those who admit the possibility of metaphysics, of significant talk about Ultimate Reality, and yet, because they deny the metaphysical significance of worship, do not believe in God. To say that God is real is to say, first, that we can talk about ultimate reality, Being itself; and, second, that we can properly give this ultimate reality the name 'God'.

I say that 'God' is a name, and this immediately suggests that it is proper to speak of him in personal terms. Earlier on I described the response of worship as a response of love, trust and gratitude based on the recognition that ultimate reality itself is loving, trustworthy and gracious. This also is personal language. How can such personal language be justified? Is it not anthropomorphic, and is it not ruled out by the impersonality of what we call the natural world?

These are hard questions, demanding a sustained discussion. I must, however, content myself with the briefest of comments. The Christian believer describes God as Father of Jesus Christ. In doing this he is saying that his response of worship and his belief in God is in some way mediated to him by Jesus Christ, and that the character of God is best described in terms of the character of Jesus Christ. As the Son is, so is the Father. Jesus himself provides the most adequate category for describing ultimate reality, just as he mediates the most appropriate response to ultimate reality. Thus the Christian believer is led to confess, again with the Bishop of Woolwich, that 'the man who believes in God, as defined in Christ, believes that in the unconditional constraint of love he encounters some-

[1] In *Encounter*, October 1963.

thing that speaks to him not simply of his own deepest self, nor of what he would like to make true, but of what most profoundly is true of Being itself. . . . What distinguishes the believer from the atheist is this utterly personal, gracious and unconditional relationship in which he knows himself held.'[1] It is because of the nature of this relationship that the Christian speaks of Being itself in personal terms, and dares to address it as 'Father'.

But does Being itself respond like a 'Father'? Is there any evidence of its Fatherliness in nature or in history or even in human relationships? Is not the Christian response of worship a snare and a delusion? It is the stark, ugly, cruel fact of evil which encouraged the qualified subjectivist to remove his God from nature and history and to try to preserve him in an ark of human relationships. If we cannot finally accept his solution, for the reasons which I have already briefly sketched, if we consider that the development from the earliest existential confession of Jesus as Lord already contained in itself the later cosmological assertions of the presence of Christ in creation, if we agree with J. M. Creed's remark, quoted by Professor Mac-Kinnon in his preface to the Fontana edition of that little classic, *The Divinity of Jesus Christ*, that 'to say that Jesus is Lord and Christ is not and never has been simply another way of recording the direct impression of his personality . . . [but is] an affirmation of faith about God, Man and the World, no less than an affirmation about the historic Jesus of Nazareth himself'; if all this is implied in Christian belief, how can we look evil in the face and still believe?

I admit that I know no complete answer to this question. Since this is so, such faith as I have is never secure from the arrows of doubt. If at the present moment I cannot

[1] In *Encounter*, September 1963.

help but worship and believe in God, in a response which, I hope, engages my mind as well as my heart and will, nevertheless there may come a time when I shall be converted out of my belief, when, for example, the force of evil seems intellectually and morally more urgent than the presence of God. It is of the essence of Christian assurance that it springs from faith, and it is of the essence of Christian faith that it cannot guarantee itself.

The intellectual answer, if there be an answer – and if the Christian faith is true, there must somewhere be an answer – must, I suspect, take two things into account. First, it will take seriously the resurrection of Christ and the belief in eternal life. It is, oddly enough, a biologist, W. H. Thorpe, who in his recent Riddell lectures reminds us modern theologians of the importance of this belief: 'Eternal life is, of course, a concept which is absolutely fundamental to Christian belief and teaching. Take this away, and what is left could hardly be called Christianity.'[1] And second, it will have to provide us with a new concept of the divine creativity, interpreted by the knowledge of God's manner of activity afforded us in Jesus Christ. When God creates, he creates in the same manner as he redeems – not by the fiat of sheer omnipotence, but by the condescension of love. The Infinite must withdraw a step, if the Finite is to breathe. Love must relinquish if Love is to bind.

These bare allusions to eternal life, without which the human story becomes a bubble on the cosmic sea and individual men count for no more than passing episodes, and to creative love, which allows the travail of the universe in order that it may give birth to the glorious liberty of the children of God, do not remove the burden of evil from the

[1] W. H. Thorpe: *Biology and the Nature of Man*, p. 104.

Christian intellect. They are not everything that can be said or needs to be said. My sole purpose in referring to the problem of evil is simply to show that the believer does find evidence counting against his belief and, unless he can come to terms with it in a way which at least eases the pressure of the problem, he may be forced to conclude that his basic apprehension of God through Jesus was in fact a misapprehension.

There are many reasons why a believer might find himself constrained to abandon his belief. For example, he might come to believe that the historical evidence for the life of Christ could not bear the weight of response placed upon it. Or he might make the conscientious judgement that euthanasia was in certain circumstances a moral duty, and if he believed that euthanasia was in all circumstances contrary to the will of God acknowledged in Christ, he would be compelled to balance his sense of duty against his religious belief. When therefore, it is said that faith in God expresses only a commitment, and not a belief, because it is compatible with anything or everything, this is simply not the case. Christian belief is as vulnerable as was Christ himself.

On the other hand, there are things which count for belief, and which confirm the believer's confidence in the reliability of his basic apprehension. Although some situations arise which seem to tell strongly against his faith, there are others in which the initial apprehension, which has its origin and norm in Jesus Christ, is renewed. He comes across signs of God's gracious presence to which he had previously been blind. These are indeed signs and not proofs; and they are signs to the believer and not to the unbeliever. But that is their nature and not their failing. Eggs and bacon and clean clothes and a tidy house are signs and not proofs of a woman's love – they might be merely the work of an efficient housekeeper or a progressive landlady – and they are signs of love only to love's discerning eye.

Another point to be remembered is that the believer is not alone. His apprehension is shared by others, and in the believing community – which is not necessarily the self-deceiving community – his insights and inferences are analysed and checked, and a Christian *Weltanschauung* developed, in which sense is made of life's variegated features. As there is no science apart from a scientific community, so there is no theology apart from a believing community.

Finally, there is what I shall call the test of 'fruitfulness'. Does this belief, which claims to embody the most adequate human response to what is ultimately real, strengthen the believer's regard for truth of every kind, increase his reverence for facts of every kind, sharpen his moral sensibility and deepen his compassion? This is perhaps the most searching and telling test of all. If there is a Spirit of Truth and Love, one may surely expect it to bear fruit!

Nevertheless, if belief in God is tied to a specific response of worship, then theology is in an important sense circular. It does rest on a special apprehension. The truthfulness of this apprehension needs to be tested against every kind of experience, but we cannot dispense with it. It is impossible to prove the existence of God unless you introduce his existence into the premises. There is no line from not-God to God on which a train of thought can carry us from our starting-point to our destination. To admit this may seem to open the flood-gates of irrationalism and to suggest that all argument is useless. This depends on the use to which you are putting it! What I have said about theology is in principle no different from what has to be said about ethics. Moral argument, too, is circular and rests on a special apprehension, namely, that of the moral 'right'. You cannot deduce a moral duty from an observed fact. Nevertheless the notion of duty, if it arises at all, arises out of observed facts. So, too, I suggest, belief in God, if it arises at all, arises out of observed facts, and belief in the Christian God arises out of the observed facts concerning Jesus. If you wish to stress the discontinuity, you speak of the leap of faith or of intellectual conversion. If you wish to stress the continuity, you speak of a movement of dialectic. Coming up against persons as well as things may take us from the circular language of technology to the circular language of morality; taking our neighbour really seriously may take us from the circular language of morality to the circular language of religion, from belief in our neighbour to belief in God. However, dialectic does not stick to one way only; it has several routes along which it can travel. Thought is not always unilinear, and life is not always lived in separate compartments.

'Poor, talkative little Christianity,' wrote E. M. Forster. I take his point. Christianity is not a talk to be talked, but a life to be lived. If the knowledge of God is primarily a right relationship to reality, if life *in* the truth is more fundamental than knowledge *of* the truth, if it is the man who does the will of God who will learn of the doctrine, if indeed it is possible to love God before believing in him, then it is reasonable to suggest that the interpretations of Christian belief in God which I have been discussing have one concern which may provide a common ground for further exploration. That concern is for the perspective and person of Jesus Christ. Taking Jesus utterly seriously is the point from which any Christian dialectic must begin. To some such a concern for Jesus is a sign of neurotic obsession. If this is so then let the psychiatrist heal us of our Christian sickness. Should he, however, pass us as relatively sane, then let the New Testament scholar help us to understand what are the facts which prompt us to ascribe to this man a status which, whether human or divine, is certainly unique.

HAS PSYCHIATRY REPLACED RELIGION?

by

D. A. Pond

I begin by reminding you of some of the differences between psychology and psychiatry. The former, as an academic subject, is concerned with the behaviour of man and animals, and with the activities of the mind. The subject as taught in the universities tends to be heavily experimental, and one student of it recently assured me that the degree course that he was pursuing had nothing to do with human nature! Psychiatry, on the other hand, is that branch of medicine dealing with investigation and treatment of the mentally ill. A psychiatrist has a medical qualification; a psychologist probably has not. Many might therefore object to my discussing the relevance of a subject that is concerned with the abnormal. However, it is easy to see the transformation in our physical health in the last hundred years that has come from the study of the causes and methods of control of many physical diseases. Society now gladly – sometimes almost too readily – accepts the authority of the medical doctor, as, for example, regarding diet, immunizing injections, and so on; though apparently not in other ways as, for example, about the dangers of smoking. The knowledge that enables us to have so many healthy children and to be physically fit to a much greater age has come from a study of the diseased. The same might be true of much modern psychological knowledge, but in a rather different way, as the causes of most mental disturbances are different from those of physical disturbances and the implications of mental illness for normal people are quite different. Moreover, the very concept of mental illness is a vague one with indefinite boundaries that have perhaps gone on expanding rather too fast in the last few years. One of the themes of this lecture is, in fact, a very ancient one; namely, the equivocal position of the mentally ill in society.

At the present time we have our National Health Service fully committed to the care of the mentally ill, so the methods of investigating their disturbances and the framework of their treatment may appear to be finally settled. But the position of the psychiatrist amongst physicians is still unclear. Our concepts and methods of working often appear strange to other doctors. The usual categories of medical thinking about the causes of illness, such as inflammation, degeneration, new growth, and so on, have little relevance to the causes of most mental illnesses. Likewise, the conventional treatments, such as medicines, drugs, surgery, and so on, have but a small place in the management of mental illness. What psychiatry owes to medicine is not such categories of thought, but the fundamental attitude of the scientific physician who is trained to make accurate observations, weigh evidence dispassionately, perhaps devise an experiment to prove or disprove hypotheses about patients' disturbances – while at the same time he never forgets the overriding ethical demands of the doctor/patient relationship. These attitudes born of centuries of tradition are indispensable when trying to help another human being by the light of some special knowledge.

Psychiatrists and physicians are, of course, continually brought face to face with various aspects of the body/mind problem. We know that there is an association between certain symptoms and disorders of particular areas of the brain. We recognize the genetic tendency to this or that form of disturbance of behaviour particularly in the case of the rarer and usually more severe forms of mental illness, the psychoses such as schizophrenia. Also, every doctor knows that patients' attitudes to any physical illness, such as pneumonia or an injury, greatly modify the course of the illness, though we know nothing about the ways this happens. We rely mainly on the traditional doctor/patient relationship to make best use of this natural will to get better, without either analyzing it too closely or calling in the psychiatrist to help. The exact relationship between the brain and the mind eludes us and we have to get on as best as we can with some sort of uneasy dualism, operationally defined and without any metaphysical trappings. In practice, our main effort is directed not towards these abstruse philosophical problems, but to trying to understand purely psychological disturbances. By this term I refer to the disorders that are often called neuroses or personality disorders. The presenting symptoms may appear to be the result of bodily disturbances – palpitations or aches and pains or difficulties in movement; or the patient may be aware of purely mental upsets, such as panic attacks or compulsive thoughts. Most important of all, but perhaps only dimly perceived by the patient – at any rate, in the beginning – are the disturbances in interpersonal relationships which may show themselves in rows and upsets or social withdrawal, and in turn these may cause the close relatives, who are the butt of these disorders, to react accordingly in some way. Our method of tackling them is to try and understand the interconnection of events in the patient's life. We have a biographical rather than a classificatory approach, though the latter may have its uses especially as regards prognosis. We are concerned with the effects of such things as love and hate, fear and rage, intolerance of frustration or anxiety, and thus have an attitude to human nature which is essentially an extension of the everyday approach. Our understanding of mental illness is mainly based on trying to understand its development; we are particularly interested in the way that early experiences may appear to cause subsequent psychological disturbances. This approach may seem subjective and purely descriptive, but it is adopted for the simple and very good reason, amongst others, that this approach enables communication to be established with the patient and one can thereby influence his life and perhaps ameliorate his symptoms.

There are a few points in the development of human personality that I want to stress because they bear on the development of man's religious beliefs and practices. In the beginning, the child is just alive and has to learn to differentiate the self from the not-self. The latter is at first the warm and nourishing mother on whom the baby is passively dependent. Slowly, an individuation occurs, the child becomes less passive and is able to demand satisfactions; its world remains essentially egocentric, but increasingly peopled with others. Later he or she has to come to terms with peers in the family and at school. Gang life, of one sort or another, is a very necessary stage of development. In education and later in employment, the child becomes the young adult, aware of people below as well as above him as he rises up the hierarchy with increasing opportunities of exercising power and influence. In these relations he has to replace his egocentric thinking with greater self-awareness and awareness of others' needs. The most difficult of all relationships at this mature, adult level are, of course, those found at marriage and parenthood, as marriage is by far the most intimate and long lasting of all our adult experiences. Even for those who are unmarried, family life is experienced in one way or another and it tends to be a norm against which all other adult relationships are measured.

Religious behaviour and experiences can be thought about in a fashion similar to other human actions and experiences, though there are certain obvious difficulties. One's relationship to God is unique; its description can at best only be analogous, but religious development goes through phases that are parallel to the development of many human relationships. Passive dependency on an omnipotent God-the-Father is found in many adults. The child's apprehension of God-the-Father will be very much conditioned by his own parental experiences. This does not mean that the popular and over-simplified view of Freud's theory is correct, namely, that God is merely a projection of one's own father. It will only be so if one has locked up one's religion in infantile prayers and habits and makes no effort to grow in this relationship by sharing the religious experience of others, especially those of the great saints and mystics. The failure to do this is as wrong as failing to learn modern knowledge of how things work and to rely purely on childish beliefs and magic. When people fall ill mentally there are disturbances in their personal relationships, and a man's relationship to God is likely to be similarly distorted. Those who are pernickety and obsessional are likely to have a ritualistic religion. The severely depressed person may feel himself abandoned by God as well as by all other human beings as a result of his wickedness. The moody adolescent, having difficulty in controlling unfamiliar sexual impulses, very frequently tries in the crudest way to seek God's help to control what he feels he cannot manage on his own. The simple, wish-fulfilment character of much pie-in-the-sky religion is well known to everybody. In this sense religion may be neurotic and it is all the more liable to be so than many human relationships because religion is so much concerned with man's deepest feelings and emotions in the least acceptable and manageable part of his personality.

Most human relationships have an end outside the strictly personal encounter. There are examinations to pass, jobs to do, children to raise, and so on; but in these relationships there is also an effect inside the personality which may be partly deliberately induced, as when educationists talk about the importance of building character as well as of just passing exams and acquiring so much knowledge. In employment, on the other hand, the question of whether a job is soul-destroying or life-enhancing is not often considered by an employee, and rarely by an employer. Although the Church is, of course, very properly involved in a great deal of good works, this does not seem to be the real aim of religious behaviour in the same sense as the job to be done is the aim of work relationships. There is an interior aim that is expressed rather indirectly by words such as Beatitude or Seeking the Kingdom of God. The nature of this sort of more mature relationship we shall consider further, later.

It is perhaps hardly necessary for me to stress that Christianity is not just a set of rules about a way of life. It is, for better or worse, very much concerned with creative human relationships between people and between God and ourselves; particularly at the very deepest and most emotional level. Modern psychological knowledge leaves us in no doubt that it is relationships at this sort of level that are most crucial in the formation of human character. Everyone knows that psychiatry is full of oral and sexual language. This is because the primitive and very intense experiences of love and hate in the baby persist in one way or another throughout life as partial determinants in later human relationships. Likewise, sexual feelings are the deepest and strongest of adult relationships, and coping with them, for better or worse, is very closely connected with mental health or ill health. The Christian language is full of similar symbolism. We need only mention the words Holy Communion and the concept of Mother Church, which is also the Bride of Christ. These words have a literal meaning that links them with the everyday facts of human nature. This is one reason why the Gospel can be so gladly received and understood even by the most illiterate. It may also help to explain why some reject it, especially those very clever people who are very often not good at these every-day human relationships. Amongst scientists one finds that their apparent passionate concern for objectivity in their research spills over into their lives generally and results from a fear of human involvement rather than any abstract love of truth itself.

Communication at this level of emotional contact is, of course, difficult to express in words, as the experiences are so often pre-verbal in the small child. They are an essential part of psychotherapy, helping the mentally ill, the pro-cesses of which, I think, are not fundamentally different from the processes of development of normal character and personality. Education, however, also has the external aim of the facts to be learned, the culture to which the patient must adjust; whereas the therapeutic situation, whether in individual treatment or in group psychotherapy, has, as it were, only one aim and that is the purely internal one of getting the patient better by changing his outlook and even in a small way his character. The psychotherapy group is thus unique in that it has no outside aims, such as the job of work for which it meets.

What we have to ask ourselves is: What are these experiences that people have and in what language can they be expressed? This is a perfectly proper matter for scientific study which is why it is indispensable to have some sort of medical orientation, for medicine rather than psychology is so far the representative of the scientific attitude in the field of human behaviour and experience at its deepest level; that is to say, in treatment, especially as regards the fundamentals such as life and death. This scientific study is, of course, relatively new, and the history of religious ways of changing people is a good deal longer than the history of psychotherapy. For the physician, management of the mentally ill has always been a rather peripheral concern – a none too respectable speciality.

As regards their dealings with people, the traditional roles of the priest and the physician have certain similarities and differences. Both tend to be authoritarian and say: Do this, or Do that; or Believe this, or Believe that. But the doctor, in assuming responsibility for bodily dysfunctions, treats them as if they were something foreign to ourselves as patients. This dichotomy accounts for some of the difficulties that physicians get into when they try and be psychiatrists where the illness *is* the personality and the disturbance is not, as we say, ego-alien.

The priest, on the other hand, appeals directly to the personality and talks most of the time about sin and responsibility. He affirms what should be done to be rid of these disturbances. The priest has his stereotyped techniques just as much as the doctor has; but when we are in need of psychological help, what we want is a listener, not a talker. We do not want the doctor's prescription nor the priest's faith; we want to find out more about ourselves. The faith that we want is in the first place the faith that we *can* find out for ourselves, and the fear that we have is the fear of freedom that we find we have when without the authority of the priest or the doctor.

We can, I think, profitably divide up the study of the ways of changing people in therapy and in religious organizations into a study of the techniques of communication and the study of the content of what is communicated. By the former, I mean we may consider such things as the sermon, the study circle, the revivalist meeting and the confessional – to mention just a few from the sphere of Christianity. Three current psychiatric techniques are classical psychoanalysis, behaviour therapy and group psychotherapy.

By 'content' I refer to the sort of communications that are made between the therapist and the patient, or the confessor and the penitent – or whatever other words are used to describe these relationships. In all these situations the language used is necessarily in some ways symbolic or allegorical because it is a very deep and emotional level of communication. It is notoriously difficult to describe what goes on in psychotherapy because it is like falling in love – a state that is inconceivable unless one has actually experienced it, and if one has experienced it then only poetic language appears to be able to do it justice. Furthermore, the communication between people at this sort of level depends much more on the emotional *rapport* developed between them than on any actual words that pass. The relationships of lovers, and of babies and mothers, go far beyond words, and artistic and poetic language is the nearest one can get to them. The real problem of trying to deal with the mentally disturbed is not whether it is illness or sin that worries them, nor whether they need help from a priest or doctor, but who is it that can give a sufferer these experiences that are needed in order to be helped? Such helpers have always existed in one form or another in all societies, though the quacks always greatly outnumber the genuine healers. The medicine man, the oracle and the prophet are such people, and they occupy a curious fringe position in society. What they do is usually done in private and in secret, and their published works, if any, are usually deliberately obscurantist. The Old Testament and Greek literature are, of course, the main ancestors of our western civilization in this regard. The truth of their insights is well brought out by the way psychoanalysis was able to appropriate unchanged so many of the Greek notions such as the Oedipus complex. Contemporary psychology, however, is no longer content to accept these ideas as just eternal truths or archetypes to be verified again and again in patients' fantasies, but it tries to understand how they originate and how they can be controlled, which is not the same thing as 'explaining them away'; nor will it necessarily result in their no longer being important.

Two further things should be noted about the psychotherapeutic relationship: firstly, though it has been well said a long time ago by an eminent psychoanalyst that 'the physician's love heals the patient', it is equally true to say that love is not enough on the part of the physician. To be able to help people requires much self-consciousness and self-understanding, and a disciplined habit of mind that can only come through having been oneself through the experience of being helped. The second thing to notice is that only a person wanting to be changed is willing to enter into this sort of personal relationship and be influenced by it. Many a patient prefers to hang on to his symptom rather than get better, and we are all aware how few people are ready for religious conversion. Psychotherapy is time consuming and tiring. It means sometimes giving up a lot of very nice things and learning a lot of very unpleasant things about oneself. People do not enter into it unless the pain of their symptoms to themselves and others is so great that they really do want to be changed. Much the same considerations apply to a man trying to follow the Christian way of life.

The patient or the convert has to feel that someone cares sufficiently for him to make it seem worthwhile giving up an old adaptation for a new one. The process is psychologically similar in many ways to the way in which a baby learns self-control, especially as regards habit training, feeding times and control of bowels and bladder. The regulation of these pleasures by giving up their immediate gratification when hunger or bodily discomfort occurs, comes about if the child feels that it retains, as a result of learning this control, the love and approval of its mother. The Christian does things not for any selfish egocentric motive, nor from any fear of endangering an immature dependency whether on parents or God, but 'because God first loved us'.

So far we have talked mostly about the human situation that may need to be changed, and the methods of changing it. Can anything be said about the desirable end-product? Much has been written by psychiatrists about the character of the mature adult, but it must be made clear straight away that this desirable state is rarely, if ever, reached by psychotherapy. From its very nature psychotherapy is a purely voluntary relationship which people can leave at any time, and they often do leave long before a desirable end is reached, and everything that could be done for the person has been done. It is firstly important to realize that the mature person will not always be a happy one. Freud, himself, never far from the realistic and pessimistic view of human nature that is so well set out in the Old Testament, said that the effect of psychotherapy was to substitute for neurotic misery human unhappiness. The way of the Cross is not far from this point of view.

It is a commonplace observation that in our society man is trying to achieve a degree of self-consciousness and self-determination never before attained. All those who have lived and worked in more primitive societies find that there is much less clear differentiation of a man from his family and from the wider circle of his tribe than in our society. The most recent and one of the greatest periods of increase in self-determination was, of course, the Renaissance, when man, to a greater degree than ever before, seemed to be able to free the world outside himself from the projections of his own fears and desires and thereby be able to study it more dispassionately. This sense of freedom is now being extended into ourselves. The freedom of which I speak is not so much in the political sense, but in the psychological sense of people having to find out much more about themselves and about how to live their personal lives. Yet this individuation is balanced by an even more important growth in our understanding of the way in which we do, in fact, inevitably belong one to the other. In psychiatry, as I have already mentioned, one hears a great deal about childish attitudes of dependence, and so on. The mature adult-to-adult attitude, whether it is man to man or man to woman, or man to God, has never been better summarized than in Martin Buber's famous book, *I and Thou*. The perfect I–Thou relationship to God is in an important sense the

Christian ideal. It is something unique and therefore difficult to talk about. Like other personal relationships it can be impaired in so far as one's own needs and problems get projected upon it. The New Testament is full of the phrases that we must have all heard a hundred times describing the perfect love that is found in the Christian relationship to God. That these phrases have all now becomes clichés is one of the difficulties against which we all struggle. Words, even poetic words, lose their emotional power. Artistic fashions come and go, very rightly as human creativity continues, and religious symbols share in this normal process of decay of most symbolic language used for human communication. We know, for example from history, that simple and great questions such as 'Are you saved?' really did cause people to change their mode of life. Nowadays we have to wrap it up rather more cumbersomely.

The Christian rightly places great stress on the need for personal responsibility, and an increase in such responsibility is also a desirable end-product of psychotherapy. It is paradoxical that the ordinary scientific determinative approach to phenomena, such as dreams that were formerly thought to be irrational, has resulted in techniques that definitely increase man's responsibility. There is no time for me here to go further into this apparent clash between determinism and responsibility.

Closely allied to the problems of responsibility and indirectly to that of happiness is the problem of guilt. There was a time, now long since passed, when psychologists were supposed to free people from all sense of guilt. Guilt was put down to all sorts of complexes, or to a harsh super-ego, and it was all too easily assumed that if one did what one liked, then no guilt would result. In contrast, a clergyman was supposed to make you feel guilty in order to get you to come to church and do what he wanted. As so often in this sort of argument, difficulties arose from the different use of words in different situations. For the lawyer guilt implies an offence against the law; for the moralist an offence against certain principles; for the theologian a sin, an offence against God. For all three of them it is an objective condition arising from a departure from some standard. On the other hand, psychologists and psychiatrists use the word guilt, not for such an objective situation, but to describe a subjective emotional state – a sense of wrongdoing – that need not necessarily arise when the law or morals are transgressed or a sin committed. On the contrary, it is very frequently present in people who are apparently blameless in all these respects. Such a guilt sense arises in some way or another from an ingrained psychic conflict, from something going on, for the most part unconsciously, in the patient's own mind. To this extent, therefore, the sense of guilt *is* unhealthy, but it is a good thing to the extent to which it may be related to the actual transgression of some law or principle. What we need to find out is a means whereby a proper sense of guilt and responsibility can be attached to the right sore of abberations of behaviour. We have to free people of a paralysing and irrelevant sense of guilt that is early inculcated in the human personality, thereby preventing further maturation. One of the difficulties is, of course, that, certainly as regards the law, people are classed as responsible or irresponsible; witness, for example, the frequent and unedifying legal psychiatric arguments in murder trials. But as Baroness Wootton, amongst others, has pointed out, deciding whether a person is responsible or not has nothing to do with the rational decision on the correct way of dealing with the criminal. It is usually more instructive to try and find out why this man disobeys a rule of which he is perfectly aware and whose rightness he would probably accept.

Another important point about the mature person concerns the role of faith in his life. We are supposed to be living in a sceptical age with mocking doubts of the value of any faith – an attitude which seems to satisfy the need for scientific detachment, and at the same time to be smart and sophisticated. This cynicism shows itself in various ways – in distrust of organization, as well as distrust of deep personal contacts. It is seen in all social classes and at all levels of intelligence. Yet the need to give oneself and to be wholly accepted is very necessary for psychological growth. Credulity is perhaps a more acceptable word these days than faith. Ernest Jones, the acute biographer of Freud and one of his closest companions, has remarked how a curious credulity is often one of the signs of the greatest men of genius. Freud himself was a remarkably bad judge of character as regards his close colleagues and he was very credulous about some of their crankier notions. Jones points out that this credulity probably is of great psychological importance as moments of identification, harmony of personality both within himself and in relation to others, seem to be a prerequisite for genius to be at its most creative. We must not, however, expect the modern psychology to tell us in whom or in what we ought to place our faith. In this sense, psychology can never bolster up, prove, disprove, justify or falsify one's religious beliefs. That in which one places one's confidence or credulity has in the end to be a personal affirmation. This carries with it its own dangers of blindness and rigidity and the pain, perhaps, that one has to acknowledge that one has made a mistake. But it is infinitely better to do this than never to dare to gamble one's life in love.

It is now time to say something about the role of the priest and of the Church as a visible organization. Of course, the Church does many important things in the world – its teaching function, its care for the down-and-out and the handicapped, its missionary work, and so on. For all these purposes, groups are formed within it with these outside aims, but we all feel that these are not the only or even the main aims of the organized Church. Rather it is a group that exists for itself as the world sees it, though, as she rightly says, the aim of man is the worship of God. We feel the priest is not only a teacher, nor is he a social worker; but in so far as he wants to alter human nature his role certainly resembles that of the psychotherapist. The trouble is that the Church has hardly become aware of the newer techniques and much of our symbolic language is worn out. The priest's equivocal position in society is brought home by the fact that there is no simple word for his relationship with the layman. We speak of the doctor/patient relationship; the social worker/client relationship, but priest/what? relationship. 'Penitent' is too technical and narrow, 'parishioner' too wide and merely topographical. No one can doubt the need for a healer or a counsellor today. The Welfare State and the National Health Service have done little or nothing to reduce the need for personal counselling and, in any case, to what extent ought the National Health Service concern itself with those who are merely unhappy or ineffectual? There is a danger that by stressing too much that a man has a mental disease like any other disease, a one-sided view of a problem will occur. Physical symptoms may be treated at the expense of the underlying problem, and the fact that the problem is so often spiritual as well, and concerned with man's relationship to God as well as his relationship to other men, may be overlooked. There is perhaps a problem here similar to that which we find in education, which, though secular, allows for religious teaching. Is it possible for the process of healing to be similarly divided up into a psychological component and a spiritual component – the two bits being treated by different people using different concepts?

One of the early leaders of the Salvation Army said: 'You can't talk to a man about being saved or about the love of God without first feeding and clothing him.' At the present time, man's problems are more of emotional starvation. 'If a man love not his brother, how can he love God?' is only too true, and it may be necessary to help people to love their fellows first if God is unknown to them as a person. 'The spirit bloweth where it listeth,' and we must not attempt to imprison too narrowly the means whereby people find God. Mere intellectual assent to or dissent from the Westminster Confession or the Thirty-nine Articles never relieved anybody of psychological difficulties, any more than believing or disbelieving in Karl Marx or the Tory Party. Healing comes from the experiences, not the beliefs, that may be both individual and in groups. If the Church is to have an effective function at all, it must as a group have some psychological meaning to the members in it in the sense that creative human relationships take place there. But the local Church group cannot be as intense as the relationships that occur within group psychotherapy. The primitive nature of the emotions and tensions within such a group are too great. A certain anonymity is essential in the therapeutic situation. One of the ways in which people can be helped with their own internal problems is by their seeing them externalized and obliquely, as it were, in the great myths which are particularly effectively portrayed in classical plays. The Greek tragedies still hold their own and can be as effective as they were when Aristotle spoke of their purging the soul. We are now recovering some sense of the sacraments as drama, a re-enacting of the most fundamental human experiences at a universal level.

The most creative human relationships are, in fact, those that can be conveyed only symbolically in the themes of birth and re-birth, crucifixion, redemption and resurrection. Patients in treatment – even quite irreligious ones – often use these words, or similar ones, to describe the psychological experiences of being changed, made a new man, having to give up what seems to be one's whole life in order to be renewed.

In recent years we have heard a good deal about demythologizing the gospel. It is seen as an effort to strip away from the gospel the accidents of its particular period of history in order to present its essential message. What we perhaps need is to *re*-mythologize the gospel so as to make out of these great themes new experiences that will again change people. For few, if any, people is it possible to relate creatively purely to an idea, and the action of the sacraments has helped many people to make that special relationship with God which enables them to deal with their own problems. These are essentially whole-person experiences, not just intellectual exercises; but, unfortunately, institutionalization and intellectualization are the besetting sins of any new movement, so that the original fire gets lost. Such a decay is already even happening to psychiatry. Psycho-analytical concepts are now part of every intellectual's stock-in-trade, but a fat lot of good it does them when they get into emotional difficulties!

In no real sense, therefore, has psychiatry replaced religion. It is a branch of medicine which embraces many methods for helping people in trouble. In the techniques of psychotherapy there are perhaps some new ideas, or at any rate an exploitation of methods of helping people that were imperfectly understood in the past. But the result of its deepest researches has shown that the themes of the great religions are still the main ones in most people's lives. It is of interest to note that Freud himself, though very much a creature of the late nineteenth-century materialism into which he grew up, began in his later books to talk in quite different terms. For example, at the very end of one of his later works, *Civilization and its Discontents*, he is talking sombrely about man's tendencies to self-destruction that could result in the total destruction of civilization. He goes on: 'It is to be expected, however, that the other of the two Heavenly Powers, the Eternal Eros, will make an effort to assert itself in the struggle with his equally immortal adversary.'

In psychiatry as such we do not have to follow Freud either in his earlier crude materialism or these later fancies which sound like echoes of his rabbinical family background. After all the centuries of religious bigotry and persecution, we should perhaps have learned that our revelation is something that we have to find out for ourselves in our own experience.

IS CHRIST UNIQUE?

by

C. F. D. Moule

At the end of his fine lecture, Mr. Baelz suggests that the interpretations of Christian belief in God which he has been discussing have one concern which might provide a common ground for further exploration. That concern, he says, is for 'the perspective and person of Jesus Christ'. 'To some,' he adds, 'such a concern for Jesus is a sign of neurotic obsession. If this is so then let the psychiatrist heal us of our Christian sickness. Should he, however, pass us as relatively sane, then let the New Testament scholar help us to understand what are the facts which prompt us to ascribe to this man a status which, whether human or divine, is certainly unique.'

Dr. Pond allows, I think, that Christians may be passed as 'relatively sane'. It does, therefore, fall to me to explain why, and in what sense, Christians ascribe to Jesus a status which is unique; and if Mr. Baelz is right, this estimate of Jesus has implications which reach out far beyond my own specialized field as a student of the New Testament.

Perhaps it may help to tie my material together if I make two assertions without further delay. The first is that the kind of uniqueness with which Christians are concerned is an inclusive, not an exclusive kind. I shall develop that in a moment. The second assertion is that the secret of that inclusiveness is, in a single word, service. That I will develop a little at once, in order to take it up again at the end.

I would formulate this point about service in some such way as this. We know that Jesus of Nazareth did many of the things that 'angry young men' are supposed to do. He challenged authority; he ruthlessly exposed the hypocrisy of the religious leaders; his behaviour, and the company he kept, were unconventional, to say the least. Of that, Mr. Wren-Lewis speaks in his lecture. What is sometimes forgotten is the constructive side of it all. Jesus combined his challenge to authority with a supreme self-discipline and an extraordinary capacity to give and spend himself for others. Through all his impatience with convention, Jesus seems not to have conceded an iota to the morals of the strange company he kept; and he maintained a remarkable faithfulness to the religious practices of Judaism, both public and private. He went regularly to synagogue (where the sermons must often have been trivial and boring), attended festivals in Jerusalem, and rose long before day for private prayer; and all this, concurrently – and this is my main point – with long days at the disposal of the milling multitudes that sought his help and his company. That is, he was anything but a merely destructive critic.

Merely to set up as a critic of convention may be inexpensive. When Jesus played the iconoclast, he paid for the damage. For his conflict with religious tradition, he paid, deliberately and with his eyes open, with the last drop of his blood.

Thus, to confine one's attention to his destructive criticism is blind indeed. But even to speak of Jesus in terms of *quid pro quo* is much too shallow. Say, rather, that the Creator in him, which Christians discern, never destroyed without giving himself in return. It is not merely that he paid with his life, like any other martyr, for having laid rough hands on tradition: far more than that – so the evidence suggests – it was with creative effect, and out of concern for others that he spent himself. In the haunting phrase, used by the Bishop of Woolwich following a hint from Bonhoeffer, he was, in an unparalleled degree, 'the Man for others'.

This strange combination of the devastatingly destructive with an uncalculating generosity of constructive self-giving is something that deserves prolonged thought. It is one of the things – though only one – that suggest that the Christian estimate of Christ as unique is not a frivolous one.

It also – as I have said – closely concerns the particular quality of that uniqueness. To this costly service and self-spending in the life and character of Jesus I must return at the end.

But, before that, we must ask first, what of the prodigious arrogance of this claim of uniqueness for Christ?

The vast majority of serious people today are certainly at one 'in rebellion against the narrow horizons of cults and sects'.[1] Tolerance has long been an attitude at least theoretically approved by all reasonable people. Indeed, most religions will be tolerated precisely until they commit the unforgivable sin of intolerance.

It is not surprising, then, if it should seem intolerable (because intolerant) when Christians do claim for Christ a unique position, and maintain that Christianity is not merely one religion among others, but, in an absolute sense, *the* religion for all. This looks like an arrogant blow, aimed, in the name of religion, at the very heart of religion.

But before we judge the issue it needs closer definition. For there are at least two senses in which the claim of uniqueness might be interpreted – an exclusive sense and an inclusive. If the claim is intended to be exclusive, it will

[1] H. J. Blackham: *Objections to Humanism*, p. 24.

mean that Christ is held to be exclusively the truth: that other religions or systems, and their central figures, are deemed false, and Christianity alone true. If, on the other hand, it is inclusive, it will mean that whatever may be found true in other religions, or in systems not specifically religious, is claimed to be included and transcended in Christ.

Both claims alike are intolerant of any notion of equality, but in other respects they differ vastly from one another; and it is undoubtedly the latter sort of claim – the inclusive – that is characteristic of, at any rate, New Testament Christianity. It is a familiar fact, for instance, that by one of the most remarkable take-over bids in history the Christian Church simply appropriated the Jewish Scriptures. It was Marcion, the anti-Jewish heretic, who tried to exclude them. Jesus himself, and Paul, and other early Christians, believing themselves to be true Israelites, simply assumed the Jewish Scriptures as 'belonging'. It is relevant to this that the idea of the fulfilment of prophesy, in its most distinctively Christian form, is nothing so narrow or verbal as the claim that mere predictions have been verified. Rather, it is the inclusive and affirmative recognition of Jesus as the coping-stone, the crown and fulfilment, of the whole edifice of Hebrew religion. You may call this arrogant if you will: at any rate it is the very reverse of exclusive.

Admittedly, the relation of Judaism to Christianity is a special case; and there are exponents of Christianity, both ancient and modern, who, while thus allowing the Hebrew tradition into the Christian system, have tried to deny any validity to other religions. Inclusive towards Judaism, they are exclusive towards the rest. I fail, however, to see the logic of this as a principle; neither do I believe it to be inherent in the nature of Christianity. That few, if any, other religions besides the Hebrew are in fact so directly on the highroad to what Christianity stands for may be true; that the Old Testament is the only non-Christian religious book now included in the Christian Church's canon is a fact; but, in principle, the claims of Christianity are inherently inclusive, not exclusive.

Indeed, St. John's Gospel represents Jesus as saying, 'No one comes to the Father except by me'; but it is the same Gospel which identifies in the man of Nazareth the eternal Logos, or utterance, of God, which enlightens every man alive. Here, then, is an immense inclusiveness: wherever God speaks, has spoken, or will speak, whether through great religious leaders – Moses, the Buddha, Mohammed – or through the findings of natural science; whatever at any time may be called God's utterance – the man of Nazareth is the embodiment of that.

Long before the comparative study of religions had become a recognized discipline, the Christians of the New Testament were declaring that what their eyes had at last seen and their hands had handled was the embodiment of what God had all along been saying and doing, piecemeal and in fragmentary portions, in Abraham and Moses and the Prophets. If God is one and, in a supreme degree, was seen in Jesus, then, all along, he must have been like what eventually Jesus showed him to be.

Thus there is a great, affirmative inclusiveness in what the New Testament claims for Jesus Christ, which, in principle, evidently involves all, anywhere and everywhere, that may be called the utterance – the Logos – of God.

That most certainly does not mean that Christians have not any amount to learn, both from other religions and from secularism. Quite the contrary! They may believe that, intensively, it is all summed up in Christ; but extensively there is much for which they will continue to go to school with Confucius and Socrates, with the followers of Buddhism and Hinduism, with Karl Marx, and with all the so-called secular systems. Indeed these, we well know, can be more truly religious, when they try to grapple honestly with facts, than the evasions of much that still calls itself religion.

This is not, be it noted, to say that Christianity is a mere amalgam, a 'syncretism', of many religions. But it is to maintain that Christianity in some sense includes and fulfils all others, and that therefore no study of any of them can be irrelevant to the understanding of Christianity, any more than Christianity is irrelevant to them. Properly understood, the claim of uniqueness for Christ concerns a uniqueness of total inclusion, not of exclusion: and that, in terms not of its being an agglomeration of pieces from all religions and from all human aspiration, but of its being the root, no less than the fruit, of them all. If that is arrogant, it is with the arrogance, at any rate, not of isolationism but of annexation: it believes that all the kingdoms of the world, logically (and because he is Logos!) belong to the kingdom of Christ and of God. How strangely unlike any imperialism known to us this world-empire is, will, I hope, have become clearer by the time I return to this claim at the end.

Inclusiveness, then, characterizes the Christian claim; and this, if arrogant, is at least not narrow.

But the real stumbling-block, as all thoughtful critics recognize, lies in attaching this all-inclusiveness to particulars – and, most of all, to a particular, to a figure of history. '. . . suffered under Pontius Pilate': that is the real stumbling-block or *scandalon* of the Christian creed. That does look scandalous. It might seem bad enough that the Jews should claim for themselves that 'God had not dealt so with any nation'. It must seem sheer lunacy when Christians claim for this man of Nazareth a unique oneness with ultimate reality. St. Augustine, in his description of his long pilgrimage through one system after another to Christ, has thrown this peculiarity into well-known relief: 'That the Word was in the beginning,' he wrote, 'and that the Word was with God and the Word was God, this I read (not, as he explains, in so many words, but in effect) in the books of the Neo-Platonists; . . . but that the Word was made flesh and dwelt among us, I found not there.'[1] No: and I have ample sympathy with anyone who finds himself alienated by this. What prevents me from throwing overboard a claim which seems so utterly preposterous is that – whether I like it or not – further examination convinces me that it is justified. It is my task then, as I have said, to look with you at the case for this extraordinary claim. I say 'look' advisedly: in a single lecture one cannot hope to examine a case in detail. All I can do, at best, is to throw down a handful of considerations for you to look at; hoping that you, of your courtesy, will pick them up and, perhaps, ponder their implications.

Before coming to questions of a more historical and evidential sort, let us look at two *a priori* objections.

First, that Christianity means a degrading submissiveness, is a familiar objection, voiced for instance, by Mr. H. J. Blackham.[2] He says that Christ 'is the archetype of unqualified submission and obedience to the will of God', and this, Mr. Blackham thinks, is something in which the

[1] *Confessions*, vii. ix. 13 f; trs. W. Montgomery, C.U.P., 1910.
[2] *Objections to Humanism*, p. 18.

humanist finds a violation of himself and of his whole experience. That I find, at first sight, an entirely intelligible objection. Yet, on reflection, does it not turn out to be something of a tautology? It is not an objection to Christ's way of dedicated obedience as such: it is an objection, rather, to a certain conception of God. If you do not believe in God at all, then by definition submission must be to man; and unqualified submission to any man – who would not agree? – must be intolerable. That is precisely the most diabolical side of dictatorship. Or again, if you do believe in God but your God is indistinguishable from a dictator, then, once more, unqualified submission is intolerable. We would prefer to keep our head unbowed, even if bloody. But a dictator God is not the God reflected in the life of Jesus. Jesus clearly thought of God as Creator and as Father; and, if so, how can it be a violation of the creature's self to conform to such a Creator's design? It is hard to imagine a greater freedom or a more truly human self-fulfilment than for man to function as the son of God that his Creator designed him to be; and to this, authentically Christian experience does, I believe, testify. St. Augustine's repose in God alone is a more active, more positive, more satisfying sort of repose than mere unattachedness.

In objecting to the way of submission, then, the humanist is really objecting to a certain notion of God, and one which, I submit, is far from a Christian notion. Besides, the humanist seems to come uncommonly near to self-contradiction when he does accept quite cheerfully the authority of collective man. He is content to allow that 'human beings become human in being socialized, and society is instituted in the rules, customs, procedures by which conduct is regulated and co-operation secured,

facilitated, and maintained'.[1] This I believe to be true, but
only because I also believe human society to be in the hands
of a Creator in whose will is our peace.

The real difficulty, then, lies not here but at the point
already defined – and to this we shall continually find ourselves being brought back – the astounding notion that it
is in Jesus that this will of God is perfectly represented
and put into effect. This is the claim we are still
investigating.

And here is a second *a priori* objection: it is intrinsically
absurd, it is said, to claim finality for a revelation of God
in a man. There are plenty of people who are ready to
recognize Jesus as supreme within the world of men so far
and to the present time. But how can we accept an estimate
which seems to place this man in a position of absolute
finality in the entire universe? What if man evolves beyond
himself into some superior creature? How can we be sure
that he has already reached the end of his development, or
deny the possibility of super-man emerging? And, in that
case, how could a man be the best window into reality for
super-man? Or suppose there are sentient beings on
some other planet, capable of receiving insights into ultimate reality: what becomes then of the Christian claim for
a final revelation in the man Jesus?

Such objections are perfectly logical. The only question
is whether they correctly represent the claims of
Christianity. The risen and glorified Christ is indeed
hailed, in the New Testament, as Lord of the universe –
the cosmic Christ. But here we are back again at the Logos
doctrine. The claim that in Jesus the Logos (God's utterance) was made flesh means, surely, that Jesus expresses,
in a human personality, absolutely all that it is possible

[1] *ibid.*, p. 16.

111

for God so to express. It does not – as far as I can see –
involve the denial that the same Logos might be expressed
in its maximum possible completeness in whatever else man
might one day evolve into. Jesus – so Christians believe –
is God's last word in man. I cannot see any contradiction
to this in supposing that there might be an expression of
the same Logos of God at any other level of creation, below
man (as we reckon orders of being) as well as above him,
or in some collateral order of being alongside of him (say,
a Martian) – an expression of the same Logos which, for
that particular level, was also perfect and final.

> ... in the eternities
> (wrote Alice Meynell)
> Doubtless we shall compare together, hear
> A million alien gospels, in what guise
> He trod the Pleiades, the Lyre, the Bear.
>   Oh be prepared, my soul,
> To read the inconceivable, to scan
> The infinite forms of God those stars unroll
> When, in our turn, we show to them a Man.

Thus far, I have tried to define the meaning of uniqueness in the context of this discussion, as not exclusive but
essentially inclusive; and I have tried to meet two *a priori*
objections by showing them to be based on misunderstandings of the Christian position as I read it – the objection,
namely, that Christ's unqualified submission to the will of
God is a violation of humanity; and the objection that it is
nonsense to predicate finality of an alleged revelation of
God in man.

May we now proceed to certain more historical and
evidential considerations about the nature of the Christian
claim?

And first, it is often alleged that what Christians say about Jesus is just wishful thinking – fantasy, arbitrarily imposed upon the facts. Mr. Wren-Lewis is arguing, on the contrary, that Christianity stands, with natural science, on the empirical side of the fence, over against all approaches – whether of so-called religion or of so-called science – which come armed with presuppositions about the transcendental, and with a ready-made metaphysic. Now, while I share Mr. Baelz's doubts (if I rightly understand him) about dispensing with a metaphysic, I can bear witness, from within my own specialized discipline, that an empirical approach is exactly what the New Testament seems to exhibit.

I do not mean by that, that the men and women of Jesus' day did not bring certain religious presuppositions ready-made to their experience: of course they did – and so, for that matter, did Jesus himself. If it comes to that (are we not tired of being told it?) none of us – least of all the humanist – comes to anything free of presuppositions. But what is remarkable – and, as I think, very important for our subject – is that Jesus was such that their ultimate interpretation of him had to run, in fact, clean contrary to many of these presuppositions. It was not as if these Galileans came to Jesus armed with dogmatic convictions that he was Son of God and Lord, and all the rest of it, and determined to have him such. Instead, they came armed with a notion of God which made it, in many ways, difficult for them to look for God in the direction in which Jesus pointed. What was most startling in the outlook of Jesus himself does not seem to have been derived from his environment and upbringing; and what his disciples found was contrary to their expectation. Their type of monotheism did not readily assimilate him; and their hopes as to what God's agent among them would look like were very rudely shattered. They found Jesus, a man among a crowd of other men, coming humbly to be baptized by the revivalist preacher, John the Baptist. When they attached themselves to him, it seems to have been, in the first instance, because of his compelling character. It was only gradually, it would seem, that they were led to declare him Messiah, or Christ – God's Anointed. He was so radical a critic of current ideas of God that, to many of the devout, he seemed blasphemous – an angry young man, as I have said, and worse! On the other hand, he so resolutely repudiated methods of violence, that, in the eyes of nationalist zealots, he seemed a dismal failure.

And even when, in spite of all this, some few did hail him as Messiah, they had still to find out that they had got it all wrong. Having identified him as Messiah – as God's Anointed – they had, through bitter experience, to unlearn their notions of what Messiah was like. Instead of imposing his will by force, he resolutely accepted secular reality – and that meant suffering. And so they had to reformulate their hypothesis: after all, thought they, he was not a triumphant Messiah-King – he was a martyr, noble but pathetic. But no: that, too, turned out to be quite inadequate as a description. Something that ensued on his death drove them to a quite different affirmation: 'This Jesus has been raised from death.'

Now, I am not capable of telling you exactly what that means. But I think I know what the Christians did not mean by it. It is clear that, by saying that Jesus had been raised, they did not mean the mere restoration of a dead individual to mortal life all over again. That, amazing as it might have been, would certainly not have signified what the resurrection of Jesus signified. And something that I think can with confidence be said, is this: that it meant a final and absolute victory over everything that death had stood for; or – more accurately – it meant that Jesus had not merely triumphed over death, but had used death and hatred and antagonism – used them creatively, so as to transform their meaning. He had created life (or God, in Jesus, had created life) out of deadly hatred. There is another thing we can say with some conviction, namely, that it was not about just anybody that the Christians were affirming this: it was about Jesus in particular. To this important point I shall return later.

Well, our natural instinct at first is simply to say that they must have been mistaken. It must have been fantasy -- fevered imagination, or wishful thinking, or the conviction, simply, that such goodness cannot die. The trouble is that such a facile dismissal of the evidence is exactly the arbitrary application of presuppositions that Christians themselves are usually accused of. What one has to ask is: Does the refusal to take seriously these undoubted convictions do justice to the historical facts of the emergence of Christianity and its subsequent history? That is the question I find it so hard to get round.

I am reminded here of the people called Flatlanders, and of the charming book about them by one (appropriately named, perhaps you will tell me) A Square.[1] In the two-dimensional language of Flatland an observer had to describe what we, in three dimensions, call a sphere, passing through his world. He naturally saw it as a series of concentric circles, widening outwards from a point, and then contracting again. Circles and points he knew about:

[1] *Flatland: a Romance of Many Dimensions*, by A. Square (Edwin A. Abbott), 3rd rev. ed. Blackwell, 1926.

but this particular behaviour of circles was disturbing, and suggested something beyond, something in a dimension unknown – almost inconceivable.

So men saw what the theist calls God passing through their human experience, freely and affirmatively and passionately giving himself to men in the name of God. What drove them to a 'transcendental' interpretation – the conviction that this man was something more – was a whole nexus of indications (especially the resurrection), which, cumulatively, said to them: Here is something right out beyond our normal experience, and yet something that insists on coming at us through normal experience. Those Flatlanders knew about circles; but they had never seen them behaving quite like that before. Mr. Wren-Lewis speaks suggestively of the way in which, wherever a real and deep relation of love obtains between two persons, there is something bigger than both. That is a striking fact; but in the records of the people who watched Jesus I find a great deal more evidence still of something that points beyond the known to the unknown; something, I would say, that cannot be contained within merely human categories. I have heard of no other man of whom just these things were observed – whose life drove its observers (and I have used that word 'drove' more than once, because I believe it is the right word) to just these affirmations.

Here was a man, ready to go to any lengths in the service of others – affirming by his life, and then by his death, that love was to him ultimately important; and doing so in the name of God. And when the point of no return had been reached – he did return. This is the extraordinary conviction that overtook and forced itself upon the men and women who had known him best and for whom his death had done its worst.

It was this series of experiences – and the sequel to them – that seems to have made the early Christians find it impossible any more to speak of Jesus as only an individual of past history. That he certainly was. That Jesus had been a vividly real individual no one among the early Christians seems to have doubted. Indeed, many of them had been his close friends.

But they seem to have found it difficult now to confine their account of him to individual terms. Something in their experience had driven them to enlarge their dimensions. He was one into whose name they were baptized, and in whom they lived and acted. It is true that the writer who is most articulate about this is Paul, and that he may never have known Jesus personally before the crucifixion; but it is well established that Paul's thinking is embedded in the common tradition of the early Church, and I think it is fair to say that the Pauline doctrine of Christ as body and Christians as limbs was reflected and endorsed in the sacraments of the Church generally.

Now, one of my professional occupations is to study antecedents and analogies to New Testament thought; and certain very interesting analogies can indeed be produced, both for the conception of individuals collectively making up a body, and for the even more remarkable conception of a single, inclusive personality, in which individuals may be incorporated. But nowhere else except in Christianity, to the best of my knowledge, is this inclusive body identified with one who had so recently and so decisively been known as an individual of history. It is one thing to say that we are 'in Adam', or even that Jacob is an inclusive figure containing the Jewish nation; it is another thing to make

117

this sort of statement of one, Jesus of Nazareth, who had been crucified only the other day.

This combination of the individual and the corporate in one figure who, at the time when these writers lived, was a figure of very recent history is, I believe, unprecedented.

This, then is our *datum:* the phenomenon of a group of people deeply convinced that Jesus had been raised to life – raised to a new dimension so that he was the inclusive person in whom Christians discovered their own lives. This is the strange phenomenon which the historian has to explain; and I do not find it easy to explain away.

But can we say anything about the actual teaching of this Jesus? Some say that, even allowing that the traditions fairly represent it, there is nothing original to be found in it. For my part I am not particularly concerned with the question of the originality of the teaching of Jesus in detail, for any claim to uniqueness for him must rest more on what was done than on what was said. The central enigma of Christianity is, as I have just said, a body of people convinced that Jesus had been raised from death, and raised absolutely: not just restored again to another mortal life, but alive absolutely, alive beyond death. It is this conviction that has to be explained away by anyone who (very understandably) finds it difficult to accept. It was not any new body of teaching that marked these Nazarenes as distinct. They were not launched on a new ideology; they had no new system to offer to the world. They were just Jews with one distinctive *raison d'être:* a conviction about something tremendous and decisive that had happened in the case of Jesus of Nazareth. Therefore, it is not essential to their position to demonstrate that the teaching he gave was unique. Quite rightly the late Professor C. S. Lewis wrote: 'You keep on discovering more and more . . . how constantly our Lord repeated, reinforced, continued, refined, and sublimated, the Judaic ethics, how very seldom he introduced a novelty . . . Nowadays it seems to be so forgotten that people think they have somehow discredited our Lord if they can show that some pre-Christian document . . . has "anticipated" him . . . The whole religious history of the pre-Christian world, on its better side, anticipates him. It could not be otherwise. The Light which has lighted every man from the beginning may shine more clearly but cannot change. The Origin cannot suddenly start being, in the popular sense of the world, "original".[1]

On the other hand, if it is true that the claim to uniqueness does not stand or fall with the absolute originality of the words spoken, it is equally true that the affirmation about the resurrection would hardly signify unless related to one whose life and teaching – whose words and works together – themselves constituted a phenomenon congruous with this extraordinary sequel. As I said a few minutes ago, the Christian claim was not that just anyone had been raised from death. The point was not merely that a miracle – however extraordinary – had taken place; the point was that this superbly good man, Jesus, whom they had known and watched, and by whom they found their own lives at once condemned and inspired – it was this man who had come beyond death absolutely. The content of his life and teaching are, in that sense, highly relevant to the central affirmation about the resurrection. And while it may be possible to adduce a parallel somewhere, from one civilization or another, to every saying attributed to Jesus in the Christian tradition (and I am not concerned to contradict it), yet the aggregate of his teaching does, so the evidence suggests, constitute something in a class by itself, for its

[1] *Reflections on the Psalms*, Fontana, p. 28.

incisiveness and its depth. Still more remarkable is the close identification between his words and deeds: he lived his teaching. Whatever may be said about the miracle-stories of the Gospels – their parallels outside Christianity or their legendary character – the stubborn fact remains that – express it how you will – Jesus has stamped indelibly upon the traditions of his ministry an impression of sheer, unprecedented mastery of circumstances. Dynamic word and significant deeds-of-power – the two together add up to what a recent writer has called 'the astonishing sovereignty with which Jesus confronted men in his words and his actions'.[1] In other words, the best evidence we can get supports the conclusion that the crucified Jew who, as Christians claimed, had been raised to life absolutely, had exhibited – quite independently of any originality that might or might not attach to a given saying – such harmony of word and deed in the devoted service of men as constituted sheer sovereignty.

We must turn now to a thorny question – the relation between Jesus and the Church; and this will lead into my closing point. The Church, it is sometimes said, invalidates any claim that might be made for Christ; the Church is a bad advertisement for its own wares. That latter remark is too true.

The failures of the Church are drearily familiar: it does not take an exceptionally conscientious penitent to draw up a tediously long confession of ways in which the Church has obstructed truth, exploited human lives, and allowed internal strife and deep division to wreck its witness. In many ways and in all ages, the Church has failed tragically to reflect the spirit of Jesus Christ. We know how many

[1] H. Zahrnt: *The Historical Jesus*, p. 112, Eng. trs. Collins, 1963.

are alienated by it today. But it would be a gross over-simplification to say, 'Therefore, I choose Christ but reject the Church.' Quite apart from the long list of noble deeds which, in all truthfulness, any impartial investigator would need to balance up again the debit account, the facts are, in any case, too complex for so simple a solution.

In the first place, it is owing to the Church's own witness that we know how far short of the standards of Christ it is falling. Whatever the Church's failings, it is to the Church that we owe the very portrait of Christ which exposes them, and it is to the Church that we owe the careful preservation of that portrait. The New Testament, which gives evidence against the Church, is of the Church's own making.

Then, secondly, for all its failures, the Church remains the means of access to Christ today. The Church's function is not merely to have compiled and preserved a written record: the Church (as Christians believe) is the organization through which and in which the risen Christ himself maintains contact with those who acknowledge him. For Christianity is not merely a body of teaching; nor is it a matter of individuals each following a great example; neither, again, is the Church a voluntary society of those who are interested in Christ. In Paul's phrase, the Church is the Body of Christ. It is the organism, rather than the organization, in which and through which God, in Christ, is found and worshipped still – finds us and challenges us still. It is impossible to be a solitary Christian, for Christianity is not mere knowledge about Christ, nor mere aspiration after his example, but organic union with him in his People – and that, in practice, means within some local congregation of Christians of whatever denomination it may be.

Therefore, however often and however grossly the Church, in all its various denominations and sections, fails, it remains the medium in and through which the corporate life of the living Christ must operate. To be a Christian is not simply to accept as true a certain amount of teaching; nor even simply to accept membership in a human society. It is to worship God in Christ and to draw moral strength from union with him in his Body the Church.

Consequently, it is simply unrealistic to say, 'I choose Christ, but not the Church.' You cannot have Christ without the Church, for the Church – represented, for a given individual, by whatever local manifestation of it he belongs to – is Christ's organ of communication. Yet neither must Christ be judged by the Church's performance. On the contrary, the Church has always recognized that it stands 'under judgement', and that the evidence which it gives about Christ is its own verdict on its own failure to live up to his standards.

But – an objector may persist – if Christ were what he is claimed to be, would he not have somehow secured that the Church should be more adequate? Such an objection betrays a total misconception of the meaning of Christ. It implies a God who achieves his plan by coercion; whereas, if the Cross means anything at all, it means that God achieves by involving himself in suffering – never by overriding the freedom of the human will. It is inconsistent to approve Christ's profound respect for personality, and then blame him for not coercing the Church into unity and effectiveness. That is exactly what the story of the temptation in the Gospels is about: it is Christ's refusal to adopt the world's techniques of coercion.

The relation of the Church to Christ leads me to my final

point, which, in its turn, brings me back to my opening remarks. I said then that one of the facts in the uniqueness of Jesus was that he combined with his devastating radicalism a supremely disciplined dedication to God and man in uncalculating service and self-giving. I said also that the Great *Anschluss* of Christianity – its claim to annexe and appropriate all other religions and systems – would turn out to be an imperialism of a paradoxical and oddly unimperialistic sort.

What I want to emphasize now, in closing, is that this uncalculating service lies at the very heart of this universal claim. That mastery of events I have spoken of, was mastery through an absolute readiness to serve, not through domination; and the unique sovereignty which resulted is, in its very nature, universal.

Particularism is an inevitable part of incarnation. If God really does act in history, it has got to be at a given time in history and in concrete persons and peoples. But exclusive particularism is not his way. God incarnate is God in the form of a servant; and the logic of service is to be inclusive. God incarnate, therefore, is God reaching out in service to all men.

And the proper test of the justice of a claim to unique inclusiveness is the degree and quality of service rendered. It is similarly that the Christian Church must test its loyalty. It was thus that pre-Christian Israel stood or fell. The moment Israel claimed a privilege of status, at that moment Israel fell from its vocation. So Peter, at Caesarea Philippi, declaring Jesus to be Messiah, is quickly found to have got it wrong, when his notion of Messiahship is in terms of nationalist rebellion. He has yet to learn the hard lesson of God's way of kingship, which is through suffering and service.

And whenever the Church has gone for power or claimed privilege or protection, then it has been missing the uniqueness of Christ. It is precisely the exclusive type of claim, which I rejected at the outset, that has so often led us on a false trail. It is only in proportion as the Church is out to go Christ's way of self-giving service, in proportion as it is outward-turned and essentially inclusive in its concerns and sympathies, that it enters into the proper uniqueness of Christ. How often and how signally it fails, and how deeply I, for one, have to acknowledge my share, within my small scale of existence, in the failure! But that does not alter the fact that Jesus himself came, not to be waited on, but to wait on others and to surrender his life as a means of freedom and fullness of life for many. That is the basis of his empire. That is what the resurrection endorsed and illuminated. And the Church, for all its folly and its failures, has never wholly obscured this unique phenomenon – the Man entirely for others, asserting by his life that death cannot extinguish this godlikeness.

I have attempted to indicate how the earliest Christians first reached their estimate of Christ, and the historical lines along which the justice of their claims may be tested. But I am well aware that no one was ever argued into the kingdom of heaven. Advance into a Christian position can never be achieved merely by intellectual assessment. Mr. Baelz reminds us of the saying from St. John's Gospel, that it is the man who does the will of God who will learn of the doctrine. The mind and the will go mysteriously hand in hand in this most intimate of processes. Evidence helps, but never compels commitment. Commitment illuminates evidence, but never places it beyond critical re-examination. Religion can never be contained and sealed neatly off as something decided once for all, because religion is not a department of life: it is the whole of life, lived in a particular way; and that a Christian can describe it as life in Christ is a pointer both to the uniqueness and to the inclusiveness of Christ.

Also available in the Fontana Religious Series

GOD, SEX AND WAR

Introduced by DONALD MACKINNON

'A magnificently honest and wise attempt to face certain of the great problems of our time.' – *William Barclay*

NAUGHT FOR YOUR COMFORT

TREVOR HUDDLESTON

'A noble book, a superb book, to be read by anyone who cares about race or human relations.' – *The Guardian*

THE TRUE AND LIVING GOD

TREVOR HUDDLESTON

'. . . a prophetic testimony to a living God . . . by one of the great figures of our age.' – *Church Times*

SEX, LOVE AND MARRIAGE

ROLAND H. BAINTON

Dr. Bainton lays before us the Christian attitude, past and present, to this important subject.

SCIENCE AND CHRISTIAN BELIEF

C. A. COULSON

Professor Coulson shows that science is a religious activity playing its part in the unfolding of God's purpose.

THE SCREWTAPE LETTERS

C. S. LEWIS

'A brilliant exposition of Hell's latest novelties and of the divine platitudes that are Heaven's unanswerable answer.'
– *Punch*

THE HEART OF MAN

GERALD VANN, O.P.

A plea for Christian wholeness in every department of life, made possible by love and reverence for everything that life includes.

LETTERS AND PAPERS FROM PRISON
DIETRICH BONHOEFFER
These documents, smuggled out of prison under the noses of the Gestapo, have a clear and shining unity.

THE PLAIN MAN LOOKS AT THE LORD'S PRAYER
WILLIAM BARCLAY
The historical background to and the precise meaning of the Lord's Prayer.

LE MILIEU DIVIN
PIERRE TEILHARD DE CHARDIN
The author of *The Phenomenon of Man* discusses man also in his relation to God. A biographical essay is included.

GOD'S FROZEN PEOPLE
MARK GIBBS AND T. RALPH MORTON
'A most important and stimulating book . . . clear and revolutionary thinking about the role of the laity.'
– Archdeacon of London

MERE CHRISTIANITY
C. S. LEWIS
'He has a quite unique power for making theology an attractive, exciting and fascinating quest.'
– The Times Literary Supplement

THE PSALMS: A NEW TRANSLATION
'A very impressive rendering. I am filled with admiration for the translators' achievements and have nothing but praise for it.' *– Professor H. H. Rowley*

PHOENIX AT COVENTRY
SIR BASIL SPENCE
'A rare attempt to see how the architect's mind works in solving complicated problems of construction, economics and theology.' *Illustrated. – The Times Literary Supplement*

AWKWARD QUESTIONS ON CHRISTIAN LOVE
HUGH MONTEFIORE
Four aspects of the love of God discussed in terms of the present day.

DATE DUE

GAYLORD			PRINTED IN U.S.A.